LIFE LESSONS FROM

THE LAND CALLED

HOLY

By

Dr. Kenneth Newsome

This book is published by Kenneth Newsome Ministries.
pastrken@juno.com

ISBN: 9798651217687

0
50 miles
0
50 km
LEBANON
Damascus
SYRIA
MEDITERRANEAN SEA
Zefat
Haifa
Nazareth
Netanya
WEST BANK
Tel Aviv-Yafo
Ramla
Amman
Ashdod
Jerusalem
GAZA
Beer Sheva
ISRAEL
JORDAN
EGYPT
Gulf Of Aqaba
SAUDI ARABIA

TABLE OF CONTENTS

FOREWARD

Father Bargil Pixner in his book "The Fifth Gospel" says that the land of Israel is another way that God used to make his power, love, and grace known to all people. Over and over again the place in which Jesus ministers or preaches or teaches impacts what and how Jesus communicates.

Having been in the land twenty times since 1976, I discover each time I am there, how much being or understanding where the events in the life of Jesus took place, enriches what they mean and the impact that has in my life. When I read the written text of Holy Scripture I read it in black and white. Knowing and seeing the place in which the event happens and reading the Scripture there allows me to read the Scripture in color. Allowing the Holy Spirit to empower my experience of both allows me to experience Scripture in Technicolor and 4-D.

Realizing that not everyone will get to take a pilgrimage to Israel I decided to write this book. Here I hope through the description of the place and reading the Scripture together, a life lesson will be found to enrich our walk in the Spirit with Jesus.

DEDICATION

I want to thank my family for encouraging me to take those trips to Israel that made much of this book possible. Thank you for the sacrifices that kept the home fires going and life continuing in my absence.

I want to thank Sari Rabadi, Freddie Satarawalla, Boulos Bawalsah, Saad Rawaad, Yael Katz, Tony Sabella, Dr. Charles Page, Dr. Stephan Vacilli, Hani Salameh, Yossi Maimon, Yossi Stepansky, and David Pileggi, and Eli Shukron for the insight, wisdom, and challenge to understand all that the land and the Book are teaching. I also thank all of the pilgrims I have taken on pilgrimages to Israel and who have encouraged me to write my thoughts down for devotional use.

Most of all I give thanks to Jesus! Without my relationship with him I could do nothing. So I dedicate this book to his glory!

1. MOUNT OF BEATITUDES

Scripture: Matthew 5-7

The Mount of Beatitudes has been revered since the early days of Christendom, as the place where Jesus preached all or at least a portion of the Sermon on the Mount. Jesus ascended the mount and sat down to teach (Matt. 5:1). From here, the crowd would be able to hear, as this area along the Sea of Galilee has natural acoustics. We see God's providential plan preparing this place for his son's sermon from the time of creation.

The church on the top of the Mount of Beatitudes is an octagonal shape. Designed by Antonio Barluzzi, a famous Italian architect, he used the fact that there were eight beatitudes which Jesus taught. Therefore just entering the church we are reminded of Jesus's teaching. Likewise, reminiscent of the Byzantine habit of commemorating a holy place by building an octagonal-shaped structure over it, Barluzzi reminds the pilgrim that this is a place which Jesus hallowed with his presence and his teaching. An interesting side note, the present church was financed by Benito Mussolini. Yes, you read that correctly, Mussolini, the dictator of Italy during World War II, paid for the building of the church.

Historically, there was an earlier church further down the side of the Mount, close to Tabgha, which was believed to be where Jesus had preached the original Sermon. No matter where you stop and reflect you can be sure Jesus taught here.

In the Sermon on the Mount, Jesus gives us a new revelation of what God expects from those in this new kingdom that Jesus was ushering into the world. Over and over the words used, show how Jesus had come as the new Moses. Yet, more than Moses, he was the son of God. The comparison of the Old Covenant and this New Covenant which Jesus was bringing into reality on the earth gives us a picture of why this new Kingdom of God was fulfilling all of Scripture to this point. First, Jesus gives us the Beatitudes – "blessed" or "happy" are those who…. In Matthew 5:1-12 Jesus tells us how to find true happiness which the world is so desperately seeking today. We will be blessed when we live out the life of the Kingdom and not the lifestyle the world presses us to live. Jesus describes a lifestyle that causes the followers of God to take a step first to follow the Law of Moses but then go a step further. As in Matt. 5:21-22, "Ye have heard that it was said by them of old time, Thou shalt not kill; and whosoever shall kill shall be in danger of the judgment; but I say unto you, That whosoever is angry with his brother without a cause shall be in danger of the judgment." Jesus requires us in his Kingdom to follow not only the letter of the law but to go beyond that and follow the spirit of the new law of the Kingdom as well. This example shows us that simply to follow the Ten Commandments is not enough. Yes, follow the commandments, but don't stop there. Live out the spirit behind the commandments and live like Jesus in the new Kingdom of God.

Jesus, also in the Sermon on the Mount, announces that he is God. Matt. 5:27-28 says, "You have heard that it was said," a reference to the law being given audibly to Moses on Mt. Sinai. Then Jesus says, "But I say unto you…" He is claiming his prerogative as the Divine One to affirm the law but to take it to another dimension. The divine, living Word is fulfilling the word given on Sinai and offering to us new life in his Kingdom, as we live this day by day.

Jesus used his surroundings to illustrate Kingdom principles. In Matt. 6:26-28, Jesus refers to "fowls/birds of the air" and "the lilies of the fields" in teaching about worry. The land has so much to do with the teaching of Jesus. This area around the Sea of Galilee is on the migration route for birds from the north heading south. Jesus was using what the people could see around them to teach them not to worry. The birds surely do not. And he refers to the "lilies of the field," the wild flowers that cover the mount most of the year. Jesus is saying look around you and see that what I teach is illustrated in the Creation itself.

The life lessons here remind us to always look around you and see what God has placed in creation that might be there to teach a lesson regarding his will and his word for our situation. Often, Jesus has a word for us but we are not open to nor looking for it. Thus, we miss his word. Look around and see God's finger writing a word in creation itself for you.

The lives we must live if we are following Jesus must go beyond simply following the law or the Ten Commandments. The Sermon on the Mount demands that those of us who are living in the new Kingdom of Christ must always go the second mile and follow the spirit of the law of Christ. Rejoice that you are demonstrating what the Kingdom is really like so others might see and be drawn by your life to Jesus.

We are following Jesus who is God. He is not just another prophet or a great teacher or rabbi. Jesus is God. He has authority and he gives that authority to us in the Kingdom. When we are living out the beatitudes or the rest of the Sermon on the Mount we are the embodiment of the Kingdom. The King, Jesus is present in us. Our lives lived under the new covenant and Kingdom demonstrate his kingdom on earth. How are you doing living out the new law of love in Christ's kingdom?

15

PRAYER AT THE MOUNT OF BEATITUDES: Gracious God, you ushered in your Kingdom by your Son Jesus. The Sermon on the Mount reflects the lifestyle we are to live daily. Help us to see Jesus as the great I AM who demonstrates your power in signs and wonders as we live anew. As Kingdom people we pray. Amen.

2. HIPPOS

Scripture: Mark 5:14-24

Looking at the hill upon which Hippos is located the terrain does look like a horse. Thus, the meaning of the city's name. Hippos, one of the largest cities in the Decapolis, a group of ten Greco Roman cities that were allied with one another for trade and security, sits high above the Sea of Galilee. It is a large city with all the accompanying pleasures that were to be found in the pagan areas – large theaters, temples to the Greek and Roman gods, bath houses – but that were seen as unclean to a Jewish person.

In the Gospel of Mark 5:14, the owners of the swine who died after Jesus cast out the demons from the man, come immediately to confront Jesus for what he has done. The closest city to the site of the miracle of the demoniac is Hippos. Is it too much of a stretch to believe that the owners had come from that city? More so, in Mark 5:18-20 the man from whom Jesus cast out the demons asks to stay with Jesus. However, rather than granting his request and telling him to come and follow me, as he had so many times before, Jesus tells him to "Go home to your friends, and tell them the great things the Lord hath done for thee" (Mark 5:19). We know that the man goes to the Decapolis. Did he go to Hippos or Gadara or one of the other cities? We do not know. However, we do know that the demoniac did go and tell his friends. I would suggest that the "friends" Jesus referred to were probably from Hippos. They probably had left him food from time to time. Or had tried to keep him from hurting himself as Mark refers to the fact that even chains could not hold him (Mark 5:4). Therefore, I suggest that the first place the demoniac went was to Hippos for food, clothing, and to tell of the great works that God had done through Jesus.

Dr. Robert Fischer, a friend who is now with the Lord, believed that two of the first places that persons gathered and continued to gather because of what Jesus had done were Kursi and Hippos. He pointed to the Tau cross, one of the earliest types of crosses used by followers of Jesus. It had the shape of our letter T. Above the church at Kursi and in the churches at Hippos, the T can be seen carved everywhere. I would suggest that the work of the demoniac made him a very successful evangelist. He simply told his story of what Jesus had done for him. And even to this day, reminders of the story of Jesus and the power of his work, life, death, burial, and resurrection can still be seen 2000 years later.

The life lessons at Hippos begin by remembering the power of the witness of one person who has been touched by the miraculous healing power of Jesus. Hippos, when excavated, was filled with churches. One church seems to be an early synagogue church complete with a mikveh (a place of Jewish ceremonial washing), not a baptistery. Yet the Tau cross is everywhere. We know that the structure could not be a normal synagogue. Jesus commanded that one man to go and tell his story. Don't ever forget what the power of one person's story of how Jesus has changed them and their life situation can do. Your story has power! Power to change lives, communities, and even the world. With whom will you share your story today? Where will you share your story today?

PRAYER AT HIPPOS: Lord Jesus, bind the evil in our lives. Free us to go and tell everyone of your great power that has worked in our lives. Help us, oh Lord, to be a messenger of Good News. In Jesus Name. Amen.

3.   BAY OF PARABLES

Scripture: Luke 5:1-3

Between Capernaum and Peter's Primacy is a natural cove. It is a place of protection from the storms in the Sea. It was a place to wash nets after a long night of fishing.

The Scripture in Luke 5 finds Jesus walking along the Sea of Galilee followed by a large crowd. Jesus asks Simon Peter for the use of his boat. Peter pushes the boat out a little and Jesus sits down in the boat to teach. In the first century when a rabbi was sharing with a group of disciples or followers/learners they would sit down to teach. Odd that now we stand to teach most often. My, things have changed! When Jesus taught there, hundreds and possibly thousands had come to hear. How could Jesus do it? Did he just perform a miracle and everyone heard? No, God had provided at creation for this moment for his Son. In creation, the Bay of Parables had been so designed that when at water's edge, the upward slope away from the Sea forms a perfect amphitheater. The voice of one talking naturally carries so that persons some 250 yards away can still hear perfectly.

This beautiful cove teaches us a life lesson that we need to remember and apply. God has already prepared what we need and it is available for us when we need it. The providence of God is so often forgotten. In a self-centered, self-absorbed world if we don't do it, it doesn't get done. But God has gone before us. He has prepared for our every need. We overlook God's providence. Slow down and listen for God speaking. Open your eyes to see the "boats" God already has in place for you so that you can fulfill God's perfect plan for your life.

PRAYER AT THE BAY OF PARABLES: God of all creation, you prepare the world so that we might see your power and experience your miracles. May the stories you told shape our lives so we might be used by you as well. Amen.

4. KURSI

Scripture: Mark 5:1-20

The site of Kursi, found on the northern shore of the Sea of Galilee, has been the traditional site for the healing of the demon-possessed man from Gadara. The site today has a beautiful ruin of a church complex that dates to the Byzantine period. I served on one of the digs at this site and saw the great complex for pilgrimage that was developed here after the time of the resurrection and beyond.

The encounter of the demoniac and Jesus at this place is fascinating. Jesus had come to the "other side of the lake." A phrase used in the first century around the Sea of Galilee to identify that one was going to the Gentile or Pagan side of the lake. In this Pagan land Jesus is met by the demoniac who is naked, cutting himself, and living in the tombs. The area here has ancient cave tombs and the rock has a lot of flint in it. The flint could possibly have been used to make the tools used to cut himself as mentioned in Mark 5:5.

The man with the unclean spirit cries out to Jesus to "not torment me" (Mark 5:7). Quickly, the compassion for the demoniac and the power of Jesus the Christ for deliverance from evil is seen. Jesus commands, "Come out of this man, thou unclean spirit" (Mark 5:8). Jesus commands the demon or unclean spirit to say his name and he cries out, "Legion" (Mark 5:9). Scholars have argued whether legion is the proper name of the demon or how many demons were actually present. No matter which, they cry out for Jesus to not send them from the country – a place of pagan belief and demonic activity, the Decapolis. Jesus sees the swine feeding near that place and casts the demons into the swine. They immediately leave the man, possess the pigs, run into the Sea, and drown (Mark 5:10-13). Why did the demons drown the pigs? Because to be released into the dark, watery depth of the lake was a place of darkness and evil according to the legend of the first century. It makes perfect sense.

The life lessons at Kursi are several. First, when we are bound by evil habits such as alcohol, drugs, sexual immorality, cursing, or fettered and chained by idolatry, coveting, lying, or our bodies are being cut and mutilated literally or by the words of those around us, there is HOPE. Jesus is the power that breaks evil habits, the chains that hold us, and the words and things that cut us! Second, cry out to Jesus in the midst of your struggle with evil. He will hear you and he will respond to set you free. The power of Jesus is above all and sets the captive free. Third, when you are fighting evil or the demonic, be like Jesus. Mark 5:8 reminds us to COMMAND and take authority over the devil, the defeated foe. Often when we try to deal with evil in our lives or the world, we slink back and cower. But Jesus sets the example for life. Take authority, command the devil and evil itself to be gone, because Jesus has won the victory already and he is the vanquishing Lord.

PRAYER AT KURSI: Almighty God, send your Holy Spirit into our lives and set us free. In the name of Jesus, free us to be an instrument of your power in the world. Amen.

5. PETER'S PRIMACY

Scripture: John 21:1-21

Along the western shore of the Sea of Galilee, there is an outcropping of rock. It has been shaped into stairs along the seaside. Inside the Franciscan Chapel the outcrop of rock is called the "Mensa Christi" or the Table of Christ.

The disciples had returned to go fishing after the resurrection. They fished all night and caught nothing. Jesus calls to the disciples and encourages them to cast their nets on the other side of the boat. Being trained fishermen they obeyed the stranger even though this meant casting into the deep. The Sea of Galilee is so clear that fishing is done at night and in the shallows so that the fish cannot see the nets, the fishermen, or the shadows moving above. It is interesting that they obeyed so quickly since we know they didn't recognize Jesus. As soon as they obeyed the command of Jesus, the nets were overflowing with a net-breaking load of fish. This had happened before when Jesus had called them to come and be his disciples (Luke 5:6). Peter realizes its Jesus on shore and swims in to meet him. The others follow and find Jesus already has breakfast of fish cooking over a charcoal fire. Why does John mention the detail of a charcoal fire? In only one other place does Scripture contain a charcoal fire and that is the night at

Caiaphas's palace when Jesus was being questioned after his arrest (John 18:18). Was this fire just a coincidence or a God-incident? We will see later in the story. He invites them to bring some of their catch and cooks their fish along with those already cooking on the fire.

After breakfast, Jesus and Peter are sitting at that same charcoal fire and Jesus asks "Do you love me?" Three times Peter affirms his love for Jesus and each time is commissioned by Jesus to feed sheep and tend the lambs (John 21:15-19). I'm sure the conversation at the charcoal fire was all for Peter's benefit to remind him of his betrayal three times beside the charcoal fire at Caiaphas's palace. Three times the question of loving Jesus. Three times Peter affirms his love. Three times Peter is commissioned to care for the flock of Christ.

The life lessons here are many. We can easily see the priority of love for Jesus. We could talk about the need for obedience when Jesus directs us in our scarcity and lack. But I want to reflect on the love of Jesus which goes to the extreme to help us find forgiveness from God. A love that helps us forgive ourselves and always restores us to a place in the Kingdom doing Kingdom work.

I had been struggling in my ministry for some time. I was seeking a sign from Jesus that I was still usable in his

Kingdom. I was alone and spending time at this place. I was totally alone at the "Table of Christ." I was reading the Bible and praying when I realized someone else was near me. I looked and saw a Jewish man wearing knee-length green pants and a flax colored shirt, big and blousy. I continued to pray and the gentleman came to me and motioned for me to help him light a prayer candle. I did so grudgingly, not appreciating the interruption. Going back to my place of prayer I started reading when I felt a hand on my shoulder. The man was smiling and when I looked up into his eyes I felt as if he was looking deep into my being. He patted my shoulder and turned to go. When I turned to see him, he was gone. All doors were still shut tight. I had a revelation that this was Jesus. I began to weep, realizing I was in the presence of Jesus. My weeping turned to joyous tears. A tour group started entering the chapel and I exited to continue to bask in the Lord's love, forgiveness, and healing within. As I moved out of the way and fell on my face in worship I felt the Holy Spirit say, "Look up." When I did, all I saw was a statue of Peter and Jesus. At the base it read, "Feed my sheep."

Jesus' love was so awesome. He restored me to his work in the Kingdom and he will do the same for you!

PRAYER AT PETER'S PRIMACY: Father God we love you! Like Peter we shout our love for you and your Son Jesus. Always hear us speak of our love daily as we rise from our bed. We love you, Lord. Amen.

6. EREMOS CAVE

Scripture: Mark 1:32-37

One of the most tranquil and secluded places for reflection, meditation, and prayer is a place called the Eremos Cave. Eremos in Greek means "solitary place." Mark 1:35 says, "And in the morning, rising up a great while before day, Jesus went out, and departed into a solitary place, and there he prayed." He went to a basalt cave that is located above the Via Maris, the main highway from Damascus that went all the way to Egypt. Located a little way from Capernaum where Jesus had been ministering, healing the sick, demon-possessed and those struggling with life's issues, he found a place to be renewed. Jesus had fellowship with the Father and was refreshed and renewed for a new day of ministry.

The need for time ALONE with God is the life lesson from Eremos Cave. It is here that we must realize that if the Son of God who was ONE with the Father needed time alone so must we. Coming into the presence of the Father so that we might commune, pray, praise and become refreshed, renewed, and empowered. Where is your Eremos Cave, your solitary place?

A friend of mine, Scott and I went to the Eremos Cave one evening. We found that trying to get to the cave in the dark was difficult. Maybe it was to remind us that you never find time apart without difficulty. When we finally arrived and looked out on a full moon shimmering on the Sea of Galilee we realized why this place was so special to Jesus. With the beauty, the glory, and the majesty of his Father's creation in front of him, how could he not turn to the Father? We began to pray as normal but found ourselves praying in the Spirit. Being moved by merely going through the motions, using the correct words, in the correct way until moved by the Spirit, we were praising and praying from deep within. Spending time with the Father can often be perfunctory but true communion with the Father takes the Holy Spirit moving upon our spirit and releasing the deep things within. Since that night spent in prayer, I have realized the daily need to be in the presence of the Father. I have my own "Eremos Cave" now that I go to each day. I can't live victoriously the life of faith in Christ unless I'm empowered from above by spending time with Jesus.

PRAYER AT EREMOS CAVE: In the stillness and the quietness we meet you, Father God. As Jesus needed silence so do we. Allow us the moments in life where we are still and know that you are God. Amen.

7. CHURCH OF THE MULTIPLICATION

Scripture: John 6:1-13

What do you do when you have company for dinner? That's basically what Jesus faced after preaching to the crowds. They were in a solitary place away from the cities along the Sea. Jesus realized the need of the crowd and desired to meet it. But, rather than just perform a miracle and produce bread out of nothing, he asks the disciples what they have. Jesus, even while on earth, was using human beings to share in his ministry. People are invited to be a part of the work of God in the Kingdom.

Jesus didn't ask for water as the area in which the miracle took place is called Tabgha. Another name given to the place is Heptapegon. Both names remind the hearer that this is the place of the springs – Seven Springs to be exact. There is more than enough water to quench the thirst of the 5000 men plus women and children.

Five loaves and two fish – it would have been a normal lunch for a boy. Loaves the size of a biscuit today and fish probably the size of a sardine. Not very much in and of itself but in the hands of Jesus it became a feast that fed the hunger of thousands of people and produced 12 baskets of leftovers. John's Gospel is filled with symbolism. Could it be that 12 baskets of leftovers (a perfect number and also the number of the 12 tribes of Israel), was an unspoken message that Jesus would perfectly meet the needs of the nation of Israel?

The Church of the Multiplication today is built in Roman architectural style. Inside, under the altar, is a small outcropping of rock. The earliest Christian tradition says this is where Jesus multiplied the loaves and fishes. John 6:11 says, "And Jesus took the loaves; and when he had given thanks, he distributed (literal Greek, blessed, broke, and gave) to the disciples..." This verse reminds us of another time in the life of Jesus that he took, blessed, broke, and gave – the Last Supper. Is Jesus foreshadowing an important event that will take place during the last week of his life in Jerusalem?

In front of the altar in the church we find a mosaic of a basket filled with loaves and fishes. But looking closer you find the mosaic has only four loaves in it and not five as the Gospel states in John 6:9. Why did the artist who made it leave out a loaf? Some believe because it is under the altar, that the fifth loaf is the loaf which Jesus said is his body (Luke 22:19). Others say that the fifth loaf is us. We are the body of Christ and we are now being offered to the world with the living Bread of Heaven, Jesus.

Life lessons at the Church of the Multiplication abound. There is a promise here. Jesus is concerned about our physical needs. He is not just concerned about our spiritual well-being, as important as it is. Our physical well-being is also a part of the provision of God.

We are then invited to join with Jesus in meeting the needs of the world. It is almost impossible to believe that Jesus wants us and needs us to help him in reaching out to meet the needs of the world. Yet, God has always wanted to work with humankind. We offer what we have and God takes and multiplies it. This should be a reminder to us that no gift given to Jesus is too small. Give what you have and see what God will do with your gift.

Remember we are and have the Bread of Life to offer to the world. There is no way to satisfy the hunger of those who are lost and wandering without offering the Bread of Life, Jesus. We can do this by giving to meet human need, but most of all by witnessing and offering them Christ.

No wonder the miracle of multiplication of loaves and fishes is the only miracle that is recorded in all four Gospels. Its lessons are too important to miss.

PRAYER AT THE CHURCH OF THE MULTIPLICATION: O God, you provide for our every need. As you multiplied bread and fish, remind us that whatever we have, when offered to you, is enough. In Jesus name. Amen.

8. DALMANUTHA

Scripture: Mark 1:16-20

The setting for the calling of the first disciples takes place on a point of land near the Church of the Multiplication. The point juts out into the Sea just before a small cove. Heptapegon is the place of the Seven Springs. The springs are warm water and flow into the Sea of Galilee. Therefore, fish are drawn to this location throughout the year. Being on a point, there is also a sheltered area on the other side so a fisherman could wash nets without fear of being buffeted by wind or strong current.

Jesus walking along the shoreline comes upon Peter and Andrew and sees them casting where the warm spring water enters the Sea. Jesus invites them to "Come ye after me, and I will make you to become fishers of men" (Mark 1:17). Jesus is calling persons to become disciples and follow him. Jesus is always extending the invitation. In Mark 1:20 "and straightway he (Jesus) called them (James and John)" to follow. At that time Jesus was doing what every rabbi of his time did – gathering a band of disciples, followers.

Following Jesus requires something from us. For the four disciples here in this passage, they had to give up their boats, their livelihood, even their father. It meant leaving all so that nothing would keep them from drawing closer and closer to their Master and learning from him.

One life lesson from Dalmanutha is that all of us are being called to be followers/disciples with Jesus. "…and straightway they left their nets and followed him" (Mark 1:18). Following is never easy. It demands complete commitment and dedication. To follow would mean that we must be willing to go where Jesus goes, say what Jesus says, and do what Jesus does. It is not an easy life in the world in which we live. We must respond. Are we willing to leave all and follow? From Jesus to us, it isn't a suggestion, it's a command!

Dalmanutha 2 calls us to follow. When we follow we are not alone but Jesus is with us. While having Communion at this sight Jesus literally appeared, touch my throat, and healed me so I could talk after eight months. Jesus never leaves us but is always showing up and touching our lives as he did feeding the 5000 and as he did to me.

PRAYER AT DALMANUTHA: Jesus, you still walk the earth looking for disciples to follow you. Help us to answer yes when you ask, "Who will follow me?" We follow you, oh Lord. Amen.

9. CHORAZIN

Scripture: Matthew 11:21

The fishing villages of Chorazin, Capernaum, and Bethsaida are the three cities that make up the "Gospel Triangle." Much of the ministry of Jesus takes place here.

The village of Chorazin is located high above the Sea of Galilee. If it is a fishing village, why is it so far away from the Sea? One answer could be that like modern day people, first century people didn't want to live where they worked. They wanted to get away from the grind, discover an area where they could rest and relax, not always staring work in the face.

The ruins of Chorazin are made mostly of basalt. What they used helps us understand the first century life of people. One of the excavated homes shows that they were modest and often long and narrow in width. Likewise, the homes had only one small window to allow light and air into the house. Inside, there was an arch with what looks like pass-through windows to form two rooms. Jesus's parables communicated that each time a new male member of the family was to be married he would build another room onto his father's house. When the room was finished, the builder – the bridegroom, would go and get his bride so she could come and join the family forever. This kind of construction is called an insula.

One life lesson from Chorazin helps me face death and what happens after. We have been given a promise. Jesus has gone away to heaven to prepare a place for each of us. He is the bridegroom and we are the bride, the church. When death comes to each of us Jesus will come to get us and take us to heaven (2 Corinthians 5:1). What a wonderful image for the transporting to the other side, heaven. A bride taken by her bridegroom to the room prepared just for her.

PRAYER AT CHORAZIN: Oh Lord, we know that you are always in the midst of daily life. Remind us that you empower us by your Holy Spirit to do the earthly work and the heavenly work that we are called to do. In Jesus name. Amen.

10. BETHSAIDA

Scripture: Mark 8:22-26

Another fishing village which is quite a distance from the river is Bethsaida. Perhaps the flow and depth of the Jordan River has changed. Bethsaida was not along the Sea but along the river.

Bethsaida was the home of Peter, Andrew, and Philip. It has been said that possibly Zebedee and his sons, James and John, were from here as well.

The excavation of Bethsaida by Dr. Rami Arav has revealed a first century road into the village. It is one of the places where you can definitely say, Jesus walked here. Along the road a home called the "Fisherman's House" and the "Wine Seller's house have been found. I had the opportunity to dig at this site with Dr. Arav and I unearthed a kitchen in the "Wine Sellers" house.

Mighty miracles are to have been performed in Bethsaida by Jesus. Jesus curses the city because of their lack of faith. He says that the city will be destroyed and never be rebuilt (Matthew 11:21-22). With this background, the story of the healing of the two blind men takes on new meaning. The miracle could not take place inside the city because of the curse. Today a marker has been put at the site where the city gate would have stood. This marker with painted eyes on it memorializes the two men who were touched twice by Jesus before complete healing occurs. At the first touch they see men as "trees walking" (Mark 8:24). With the second touch, sight is restored for both of the men.

Life lesson one is to never give up when seeking from the Lord. There was the need for the second touch. That means that we must be willing to ask the second time. If we don't, we will be left with only half the miracle. So don't be afraid to ASK and ASK again if necessary.

PRAYER AT BETHSAIDA: Lord, our work is to fish for people. Help us to take the time to fish in the places where there are those who do not know you as Savior and Lord. Let our lives be the bait and you the fisherman. Amen.

11. CAPERNAUM

Scripture: Mark 1-3:5

When you walk up to the ancient village of Capernaum a sign hangs on the gate that says, "The hometown of Jesus." Wait! The home town of Jesus is Nazareth. How could they claim such a thing? Jesus had been rejected by his hometown folk and he moved his ministry to Capernaum. Why? Capernaum was a border town where he could slip back and forth when trouble would arise, like had happened in Nazareth, and he would be safe. The village of Capernaum is also on the Via Maris, the Way of the Sea. This public road was a major caravan route. Being on a caravan route, the village would also have people from many different places. Therefore, any teaching given here would have the potential to be taken to other parts of the Roman Empire. Being in a fishing village also allowed Jesus access to travel to any part of the Sea. It aided him in his travels. It was here in Peter's mother-in-law's home that Jesus found rest, refuge, resources, and a place to preach the Good News of the Kingdom. Jesus chose a new hometown for specific reasons.

In the ruins at Capernaum there is a house called the House of Peter. This home, when found, was marked by Christian graffiti that dated to the first and second century.

The excavators also found signs that the house had been a place of Christian worship. Many were healed of diverse diseases and Jesus cast out many evils. Mark 2:3 describes "one sick of the palsy" who found healing when the roof of the house was destroyed to let him down to Jesus. While today a Roman Catholic Church affectionately called the "flying saucer" is built over the sight, the interior allows a full view of the ruin and the opportunity to see artistic interpretations of the events that occurred in Capernaum.

A few yards away from St. Peter's house, the synagogue of the village is found. Today, the synagogue is made of white marble dating from the fourth century. However, at the base of the synagogue, the original foundation from the first century can be seen. It is made of black basalt, the native volcanic stone of the area. Here Jesus healed the man with an unclean spirit and the man with a withered hand. Perhaps the most important teaching Jesus gave here was after the miracles of Loaves and Fishes at Tabgha. Jesus comes here and teaches the people the meaning behind the offering of bread now and the symbolism of the bread from heaven. And it is here that Jesus said of man, "except ye eat the flesh of the Son of man, and drink his blood, ye have no life in you. Whosoever eateth my flesh, and drinketh my blood, hath eternal life; and I will raise him up at the last day (John 6:53-54)."

The village was known for its fishing. Fishing boxes were discovered here that held the night's catch until it could be sold or salted or dried. Both mill stones and olive presses were crafted here from the huge basalt boulders that were readily available. No wonder Jesus talks about "millstones around your necks" (Matthew 18:6).

Fishing, millstones, olive presses, and the Sea were all images Jesus used in his teaching. Jesus was the master of using the things around him to communicate. Your life can be used to help you communicate the Good News you have to share. From Peter's mother-in-law's home and the paralytic brought to Jesus, we are reminded of what four can do that one cannot. If we do not have friends to call upon, we will never be able to do great things in life or find wholeness in life.

PRAYER AT CAPERNEUM: In the busyness of our lives make yourself known, oh Lord. We recognize that you desire us to love you as Lord in all of life as we remember. Amen.

12. SEA OF GALILEE

Scripture: Matthew 4:18

Sea of Galilee, Lake of Gennesaret, Lake Tiberius, and Kinneret are just a few of the names for the body of water in the Galilee that provides life. Fed by the Jordan River, this fresh water lake is the life blood of Israel. The water of the Sea of Galilee is one of the major sources of drinking water for the state of Israel. It measures 13 miles long and 8.1 miles wide; the average depth of the lake is 84 feet. The circumference of the shore line is 33 miles. It is a place of natural beauty and enjoyment. The Sea is nestled on all sides by the mountains of the Golan or the lower Galilee. Thus, it is like a bowl set down among the hills.

The Sea of Galilee is filled with fish. Today, as in the first century, many seek their livelihood from the fishing industry. Since the Sea is so clear, fishermen take their boats out at night and thus a good catch is normally had. However, like any fish story it isn't always a success story. In Luke 5 Jesus walks along the shore early in the morning and sees men washing their nets. They haven't caught anything all night and are now finished. Jesus commands them to push out and cast their nets on the other side of the boat. These instructions go against everything a good fisherman on the Sea of Galilee knows. The fish like the shallows not the deep. It's daylight and you don't catch fish normally in the day time here. Yet, the disciples do as Jesus said and catch a net-breaking, boat-sinking load of fish. Their obedience to Jesus's commands brought abundance.

The Sea of Galilee is fed by the Jordan River from the north and then empties into the Jordan at its southern end – the receiving and giving of the Sea.

On the Sea of Galilee storms can come up quickly. A change from a calm, shimmering plate glass sea to churning, choppy waves of six feet in height can occur in a matter of minutes. The reason for this is that the winds come down off the mountains around the Lake and have nowhere to go except over the waters, kicking up a tempest. Jesus faces that kind of storm in Mark 4:35-41. Jesus speaks to the wind and the waves. He uses the same Hebrew word that he uses when speaking to a demon to come out of the demoniac. The first century legend was that the Lake was a place for the demons. In Matthew 14:22-33 the stormy Sea is a place for Jesus to teach Peter about faith and keeping his eyes on Jesus not the storms all around him.

Life lesson on the Sea is to always live a life which is giving and receiving. When you are in the rhythm of both, life continues and is growing and life giving. The waters of the Sea of Galilee flowing down to the Jordan go all the way to the Dead Sea which has no outlet. In the Dead Sea there is very little life at all. The Sea helps us to remember to keep bringing things into your life, but also be one who gives out from your life.

PRAYER AT THE SEA OF GALILEE: Lord Jesus, our lives are like the Sea of Galilee. We have life and offer it to others as the Sea of Galilee does. Use the life-giving water of Christ in our lives so that the Kingdom might give life to the world. Amen.

13. CAESAREA PHILIPPI

Scripture: Matthew 16:13-20

Jesus takes his disciples away from the Jewish area around the Lake and brings them to Caesarea Philippi. Today the town is called Banias. Caesarea Philippi was built by King Herod to honor Caesar and enlarged and served as capital of the Golan by King Philip II. It was a Roman city in architecture and in terms of the religious life that was practiced there. Roman legend has it that the large cave at Banias was the birthplace of Pan, a god of the Greco-Roman religion who was lord over the shepherds and flocks. Also, the large cave at Caesarea Philippi was called the "gates of hell." It was believed that this was the entrance to the underworld and the river inside of the cave would carry those who were dead to the river Styx. There were large marble temples all along the face of the cliff in which the large cave was found.

Jesus brings the disciples here, and away from the crowds, asks them a defining question about who he is. From this point on Jesus will be going to Jerusalem to be handed over to the Jewish authorities and then to the Romans to be crucified to fulfill the prophesies of the Old Testament concerning the Messiah. Jesus asks them, "Who do men say that I, the Son of Man, am?" and "Who do you say that I am?" (Matthew 16:13, 15). The answers are varied as there are so many opinions due to the things he has done. They answer that he is John the Baptist, Elias/Elijah, Jeremias/Jeremiah or one of the other prophets. People could sense Jesus was sent from God and he was a spokesperson for God but they still didn't quite understood who he really was. Peter, the impetuous one, answers, "Thou art the Christ, the Son of the living God" (Matthew 16:16). It was the moment of revelation. God had revealed to Peter, the one famous for foot-in-mouth syndrome, and he had proclaimed it loudly and succinctly in front of the gates of hell and the darkness of the pagan world, that Jesus was the Son of God. Jesus uses that moment to teach the disciples and us that the affirmation of faith – that Jesus is the Son of God – is the power to defeat evil and darkness in this present age. We have been given authority over Satan and hell and death. The other point that Jesus makes is that "the gates of hell will not prevail against it" (Matthew16:18). The gates are a stationary part of a walled city, the strongest part of a city's defenses. By declaring that they cannot prevail, Jesus is reminding us that our profession of faith, that Jesus is the Son of the living God, is ultimate power over all.

A life lesson from Caesarea Philippi is that the power of our confession has ultimate power. By declaring that "Jesus is the Son of the living God," we have the power of faith to destroy the walls we face. The gates, those things like cancer, alcoholism, drug addiction, that seem to be holding us at bay, are no match for Jesus. He is Lord of Lords and King of Kings. He is the mashuah, HaMashiach, Messiah! Therefore, we are overcomers of all things in this world and in the supernatural that confront us – over the evil one and the darkness of this age. Jesus, God's only Son, is the name above and over all things.

PRAYER AT CAESAREA PHILIPPI: We thank you for the foundation of faith that is ours in the profession that Jesus is Lord. Let us hold onto that profession so that we may fight the gates of hell until they fall. In Jesus's name. Amen.

14. CANA

Scripture: John 2:1-11

Not far from Nazareth there is a village called K'far Kana. Cana was known for the production of pomegranate wine. This village has been the traditional place to celebrate the first miracle of Jesus, turning water into wine. Both the Roman Catholic Church and the Greek Orthodox Church claim to be the site where the miracle took place. In both churches you can see wine jars that date to the first century. However, Jesus did not use wine jars in the miracle but large stone pots that contained the water for purification. Jesus used that which was set apart, to allow people to come to God, to demonstrate the power of God that would draw people to him, i.e., a sign and be a blessing.

The miracle at Cana is set in the context of a wedding celebration. Held on Tuesdays, weddings were a time of celebration not only for the immediate family of the bride and groom but for the entire village. It was a time of celebration and rejoicing which Jesus and his disciples attended. The celebration would not be a few hours like our weddings, but would last for days, in some instances.

It is easy to look at the Gospel of John and see that Mary, the mother of Jesus takes a prominent place. Mary, it appears, has a role in the wedding preparations. Jesus appears to rebuff her request, yet she reminds the servants to do whatever he says (John 2:5). Mary's pure faith and confidence in her Son is seen so beautifully in her instructions to the servants.

As in other miracles that Jesus performs, he does not say anything or even touch anything, but the Holy Spirit within him transforms the water into wine, as it is taken by the faith and obedience of the servant to the chief steward. The miracle's focus while providing wine so that the host is not embarrassed, is on the power of God in the Kingdom that Jesus is ushering in. In John 2:11 John reminds us of the reason for miracles in the ministry of Jesus which was to "manifest forth his glory." The miracle points not to itself but to the God who performed it.

Several life lessons seem to flow from this miracle. First, always "do whatever he tells you to do." Being obedient brings forth the Kingdom of God and God's blessings for us. Mary's instructions should be uppermost in our minds when we are in prayer or reading the Word of God. We must have the attitude that is willing and ready to do whatever he tells you. If we are obedient we will see the miracles of God in our lives.

Secondly, Jesus loves to be a part of the celebrations. So often we only turn to Jesus when we are down or facing a situation we cannot handle ourselves. But, Jesus wanted to be at the wedding. He wants to be a part of the celebrations of our lives. Do we invite Jesus in when we are rejoicing? Remember, Jesus was always at a wedding or a party or at a dinner. Jesus loved to be in the middle of the celebrations of life.

PRAYER AT CANA: Lord, fill our lives with the joy of marriage. May we rejoice in the new wine that gives hope and life to everyone who would receive it. Help us to be obedient to Jesus and his words forever. Amen.

15. NAZARETH

Scriptures: Luke 1:26-38, 46-55; Luke 4:16-30

In the Church of the Annunciation in Nazareth there is a sign that says, "Here the Word of God became flesh." It is found in a cave which is purported to be the house of Mary and Joseph. It is in this simple cave house that the Son of God would enter into a virgin's womb, a teen who was willing to be used by God. The annunciation of Gabriel, the archangel, to Mary, the virgin from the line of David, was truly an incarnational moment. Mary's willingness to be used by God to bear the Son of God put her in great danger. If Joseph had turned away from her, she would have been stoned. What would her family do when she told them that she was pregnant and she hadn't had sex? In this small village of probably no more than 150 people, God came among us.

Another church, the Church of St. Joseph is a place to remember the person that God chose to be the father of Jesus on earth. He was an adoptive father, if you will. Joseph, we know, was a righteous man under the law. He was also a carpenter. The Greek word carpenter is translated as Teckton. A teckton was a builder. One who used wood, yes, but more than that he used stone, since it was the most accessible building material. Jesus, the builder! Can you imagine what kind of stature Jesus must have had if he was working daily with stone? His profession for 30 years seems to give us a Jesus who was muscular and in shape and not some sort of person who is not a man of stature.

In the city of Nazareth there is a church known as the Synagogue Church. While claiming to be the site of the ancient synagogue there are no first century ruins to be found. Yet, it is always good to remember Jesus reading the first Sabbath after his baptism. He came and was asked to read from the scroll of Isaiah 61 about the suffering servant of Isaiah and what the Spirit was to do through this servant. Jesus ends the reading by saying, "This day is this scripture fulfilled in your ears" (Luke 4:21).

This acclamation causes a great uproar among his hometown friends and relatives, to the point that they are ready to throw Jesus off of the precipice. Luke 4:30 tells us that Jesus simply walked through the crowd and went to Capernaum. Jesus had to be a strong man from his work but he was just a simple Jewish man. Nothing about him drew attention or set him apart or he wouldn't have been able to walk through the crowd freely. Nazareth reminds us that Jesus was as Isaiah 53:2 says, "...he hath no form or comeliness; and when we shall see him, there is no beauty that we should desire him." Jesus was just an ordinary Jewish male.

The life lesson in Nazareth is to consider whether we have the courage and faith to say as Mary did, "Be it unto me according to your word" (Luke 1:38). It is often so easy to follow Jesus when we are doing so among those who already know the Lord. However, do we have the faith to follow and be obedient to what Jesus asks of us when everyone around us is opposed to what we are doing? Like Mary, we must be willing to put it all on the line. Believe that if God asks it of us, we cannot do anything but obey.

PRAYER AT NAZARETH: Father, as we remember the first follower of Jesus – Mary, his mother – may we be like her. May we, like Joseph, be used to shape and mold lives for Godly use. In the name of Jesus. Amen.

16. MOUNT TABOR – MOUNT OF THE TRANSFIGURATION

Scripture: Matthew 17:1-8

The Mount of Transfiguration is traditionally found in the Jezreel Valley in the center of the nation of Israel. Matthew 17:1 says that Jesus brought Peter, James, and John "up into a high mountain apart." There is another site that some believe to be the place of the Transfiguration and that is on Mt. Hermon. Because of its sheer size and the proximity to the other events in Jesus's life at that time, Hermon has been put forth as a candidate for the site.

Mount Tabor is the tallest mountain in the Valley of Jezreel. It is also a historical site – the place at which the Judge Deborah and Barak fight against Jabin and Sisera in Judges 4.

One of the ways you are helped to know this is the place that Jesus must have had a spiritual experience, is that to get to the top of Tabor you must take a taxi. The zig zag road up the side of the mountain taken at breakneck speed by the taxi drivers will definitely have you in a mood to get ahold of the supernatural.

On top of the mountain you will find three churches which Peter was told not to build after the transfiguration experience. However, these churches have been saved for us and hallowed this place to reflect on what this experience in Jesus's life means.

Transfiguration means to reveal. On this mount Jesus reveals who he really is. His essence of glorious light is seen by the trio of disciples, Peter, James, and John. They see him in his glory! They also see him as he is prepared by the Father for his purpose in coming to earth. Elijah, the greatest of the Prophets, and Moses the great Law Giver, come to Jesus to encourage him for the death on a cross to which he must go to fulfill the plan of God.

Life lessons on this mountain remind us that it is often necessary for us to go apart. When we are away from the hustle and bustle, God can manifest himself to us in a mighty way. It is also when we are not distracted by life's demands that we can be aware that the heavenly hosts, angels, and the saints are close at hand. We are part of the communion of saints. Therefore, those who have gone before us are there to encourage us and help us to move on to fulfill God's desires (Hebrews 12:1-2).

PRAYER AT THE MOUNT OF TRANSFIGURATION: Father God, thank you for revealing your Son on the Mount. We rejoice in the prophetic tradition of Elijah and the law as signified by Moses to be an example for us of how to live in Christ. Let us remember we follow Jesus only. Amen.

17. MEGIDDO – THE VALLEY OF ARMAGEDDON

Scripture: Revelation 16:12-16

Megiddo is a tel. A tel is a man-made hill or mound which has risen up over the centuries by civilizations building upon each other. Megiddo was inhabited from 7000 BCE to 586 BCE. There are 26 layers in the tel. Numerous powers either built, conquered, or added to the city that was on this spot. Evidence of nations such as the Egyptians, Canaanites, Aramaeans, Israelites, and the Babylonians have been found there. Cultic places, palaces, stables, and even a water system show how advanced the life of each civilization was and continues to be in the next generation and century.

Because Megiddo stands in the middle of the Jezreel Valley. It is in the path of any nation from the south or north of Israel who uses the Via Maris trade route. The location adds to the cultural diversity that has been found in the layers of the tel.

The valley of Jezreel which lies in front of Tel Megiddo is a bread basket for modern Israel. Much of the food for Israel is grown in the valley. Since there have been more battles fought in this valley than any other, the valley has been made rich by human blood and now we know what the blood can do.

In the Revelation of Jesus Christ to St. John we catch a glimpse of the end of days. Some believe this apocalyptic literature to be referring only to events which are in the past. I believe that the Revelation is also for the future. In Revelation 16 the Vial Judgments of God are poured out upon the earth. These are a part of three sets of Judgments that are poured out upon the world for unfaithfulness and sin. After the sixth vial, John refers to a great battle that will happen with all the nations of the world participating. The place is the Valley of Armageddon, or in Hebrew, Har Megiddo. This battle will shake the entire earth. This is the seventh vial. The battle that takes place here will bring total devastation upon millions of lives from the nations of the north, east, south, and west. Some of the killing will be self-inflicted by the armies themselves. Other devastation will be by natural disaster and the judgment of God. The good news is that the battle claims the fulfillment of the victory won by Jesus on the cross. He will rule and reign in the new Kingdom upon this earth.

Life lessons at Megiddo would call us to reflect on God working through history. Nothing is happening by accident. There is a plan and God is using nations, even nations that are against him and trying to destroy his people. God can and will use whomever he wishes. When you look at what is happening in the world around you, stop and remember that our God is the God of all of history. He can and will use whom he chooses to use. Even nations that are antagonistic or destructive to God's people can be used by Him to bring His divine plan into reality. Always remember: Jesus will return with the saints and the heavenly hosts! Our God Wins!

PRAYER AT MEGIDDO: Jesus, you are the coming King. You are the one who will bring victory, riding on the white horse. Let us proclaim your victory to the world. In Jesus name. Amen.

18. CAESAREA MARITIMA

Scripture: Acts 10; Acts 24-26

The Roman governor of Palestine was headquartered in Caesarea Maritima or Caesarea by the Sea. This port city was built by Herod the Great and named in honor of the Roman Emperor Augustus. The city was built in Roman style. A large theatre, hippodrome, temples, and government buildings can be found in the archeological excavations. A thriving, bustling seaport, Caesarea was a cosmopolitan city with people from all over the world. The large harbor was one of the most well known in the Middle East at that time. In fact, Herod used a new discovery by the Romans to be able to build a protected harbor. The discovery was a cement that could give strength buried in the water of the Mediterranean.

Caesarea has given to us a pillar with the name Pontius Pilate engraved on it. This is the first evidence outside of the Bible of this governor being in Palestine.

The large Roman aqueduct along the sea was used to bring a water supply for the city. This vast Roman construction is still standing and in places still carries water, as it has for two centuries.

Acts 10 tells us of the conversion of Cornelius and his household after Peter preaches and tells them of the saving grace of Jesus Christ. While we do not have the actual house in which this took place, Acts 10:48 does tells us Cornelius and his entire household were baptized. Could it be that the baptism was held in the Mediterranean Sea? Several years ago, Scott, a friend from college years, and I were visiting Caesarea Maritima. We had read the story of Cornelius and Peter. We walked from the breakwater where we had been reading down into the waters. We realized it just happened to be 3 pm – the same hour at which the Spirit had come upon Cornelius's household and baptized them with water and the Holy Spirit. The Holy Spirit was present with us. We renewed our baptisms by going under the waters of the Mediterranean. When we came up out of the waters we were once again filled by the Holy Spirit.

A portion of the trial of the Apostle Paul probably happened in the Roman theatre. The theatre has been refurbished today and is used for plays and musical performances, just as it was in Paul's time. The defense that Paul mounts in front of Festus and King Agrippa retells his Damascus Road experience. He shares in power his defense against the charges of the High Priest and the Jews. Paul takes every opportunity to weave into his defense the Gospel of Christ. So much so that King Agrippa says to

Paul, "Almost thou persuadest me to be a Christian" (Acts 26:28).

Several life lessons can be seen in Caesarea Maritima. One would be that the Holy Spirit is still filling us today. The work and ministry of the Holy Spirit is still available for each of us. We need only be open to receive and the Spirit will fill us with power and his gifts. While there is a definite filling of the Spirit as on the day of Pentecost, there is also the constant filling. Ephesians 5:18 tells us "…keep on being filled with the Spirit." This is the Greek translation since the word for filled that was chosen by Paul means it happened but it is a continuing action. I have a good friend who says I need to keep on being filled because I leak! Leaking or just discovering more of ourselves to give over to the Lordship of Christ and the fullness of the power of the Holy Spirit allows us to keep on being filled.

I think that Paul's defense of himself also reminds us that we need to be ready to give an account of the faith that is within us, especially in the public arena. The world we live in today needs to hear the Gospel being shared unafraid and with power. The world around us is dying and is becoming more pagan in morals and culture. To share the Gospel publically in the power of the Spirit has the potential to have the same effect as Paul did on Agrippa. Sowing seeds of the Gospel by sharing our faith stories will not return to us void but will bring a great harvest.

PRAYER AT CAESAREA MARITIMA: We rejoice that you gave us a gospel for Jews and Gentiles. We are all a part of your family in Christ. Allow us to work together for your glory. Amen.

19. MAGDALA – MIGDAL

Scripture: Luke 8:1-3

On the shores of the Sea of Galilee lies a fishing village named Magdala. Magdala means "tower" in Greek. The village was known for its dried fish which were exported around the country. Likewise, the village was known as the sight of a sea battle.

Magdala was excavated in the 1970s onward. In the early part of 2000, a large area believed to be the site of another part of the village was unearthed. This time the ruins were dated to the first century CE (Common Era). Homes of wealthy individuals were found. Many including mikvot, ritual bathing places used by religious Jews. This is consistent with Luke 8:3 which says that there were "many (women) who ministered to them of their substance." Could one of these homes be one that belonged to Mary Magdalene, a woman of substance? The most exciting discovery at Magdala was the first century Jewish synagogue. The synagogue has bench seats along the walls which was the style in the first century. A large stone with engravings of the Holy Ark and a menorah were found as well. What was the stone used for? No one knows for sure but to see a picture of the Menorah….

Luke 8:1 tells us that Jesus "went throughout every city and village preaching." Thus we can be sure that Jesus preached here. The village is also probably the place in which Mary Magdalene was born or at least lived. Mary Magdalene is said to be the one from whom seven demons were cast out (Luke 8:2). Often Jesus's miracles took place in synagogues. Was this the site where Mary's miracle of deliverance took place? It doesn't matter – here we can remember and rejoice that Jesus is Lord over all the earth and over the power of evil tormenting our lives.

A new Roman Catholic Church has been built here. It has a wonderful sanctuary with an altar shaped like a fishing boat from the first century. In the basement of the church is a recreation of what the synagogue would have looked like. This is a wonderful place to stop and meditate on the miraculous power of Jesus. You could use the miracles which are recalled in the chapels of the church above. Miracles that include casting out the demons from Mary Magdalene, healing of Jarius's daughter, calming the storm on the sea, among many others.

What are the life lessons we have here at Magdala? In a lifestyle of affluence, the need for the power of God is just as real as anywhere else. We are often taught if we make enough money, get the right job, drive the right car, or know the right people everything in life will be just fine. Yet, having all these things still leave us at the mercy of the evil one. Only the power of Jesus casts out evil and evil influence in our lives. I believe there is a spiritual dimension to many of the issues we face in our daily lives. Therefore, it is imperative that we seek Jesus to cast out the fear, spirit of worthlessness, intense anger and rage, sexual immorality, among others, that possess or attack us. JESUS – the name above all names will free us from all of these and more if we only ask in faith, believing.

PRAYER AT MAGDALA: Father we give thanks for a follower like Mary Magdalene. She reminds us that even when there is dark within, Jesus has victory and offers light. May Satan be removed from our world and our lives so we can march triumphantly after Jesus ever to a cross. In Jesus's name. Amen.

20. BAPTISMAL SITE

Scripture: Matthew 4:1-11

John the Baptist, Zacharias and Elizabeth's son, was from Ein Karem. Jesus's cousin begins his ministry coming out of the wilderness preaching at the Jordan River. It isn't an accident that John came to this spot on the River Jordan. Two events had occurred here in Israel's history. This ford near the city of Jericho was used by the children of Israel when they entered the Promised Land. It was the place from which the land of Israel was ushered in (Joshua 3:9-17). Near the same spot, Elias/Elijah tells Elisha what he had been promised – that if Elisha saw him leave he would receive a double portion of the spirit of the prophet of God. As Elijah ascends he throws off his mantle and it lands on Elisha.

As John the Baptist begins to preach and call Israel to repentance he is choosing the same spot to draw in the hearer's mind that what he is doing is the fulfillment of what Joshua and Elijah had started. Baptism is the sacrament in which we are washed and called to be a son/daughter of the family of God. We are God's children and are filled as Jesus was as he came up out of the water. It is a continuation of what God had done at this place with the prophets Elijah and Elisha. The baptismal sight is a reminder that the Holy Spirit fills us just like Jesus. This same Spirit then sends us forth. Yet in our baptisms God calls us his own and then empowers us to do great and wonderful things for Him. The Holy Spirit baptizes us with power – to do the mighty works Jesus does on earth.

Life lesson one, each of us must be baptized. It is the command of Jesus. In the waters of baptism we are washed white as snow. We are publicly acknowledging that Jesus is our Savior and Lord. We are being claimed into the family of God with God our Father, Jesus our Savior and Lord, and every follower of Jesus as brothers and sisters. In baptism we are being obedient to Jesus's last command in Matthew 28. Down by the riverside, I was reaffirming people's baptism. A man who had been with us on the tour I was leading was Henry. He had been sprinkled while an infant but had never experienced nor claimed Christ as Savior and Lord for himself. I had asked him why he had come on the tour since he openly said he was not a believer. He said it was because of the price. During the tour the Holy Spirit was working on Henry. I had been sharing with Henry when I could, of God's grace found in baptism. But he had refused any conversation. I was in the river baptizing when I looked up and saw Henry staring me in my face. He said, "I want to be baptized in the Jordan like Jesus. I have accepted Jesus as my Savior and I want the world to know that I am a follower of Jesus Christ." Before he could move, I grabbed Henry and put him under the water. I left him down under the waters a bit longer than the rest just to make sure Henry would never forget what the power of God was doing in him at that moment!

Baptisms. At the Jordan it is always a joy to be able to reaffirm what has already been done in our lives by the grace of baptism. I have been to the Jordan 18 times and have always shared in baptism and baptismal reaffirmation. After all the group had left the water, the pastor who was assisting me in performing the baptism looked at me and said, "Don't you want to experience God's grace in the water?" At that time I was struggling in my personal and family life. I felt so dry and distant from the Lord. I looked at my friend and said, "You know what, I do need that grace anew in my life." He took a big step of faith. I did just that and experienced the joy of the Holy Spirit in a new and fresh way. Being renewed by the water of regeneration changed not only my heart but when I arrived home my situation had been changed as well.

While at the Jordan I wrote a song called, "Come on Down to The River." The lyrics are as follows:

Come on Down to the River

Come on down to the river, river
Down to the river to pray
Come on down to the river, river

Down to the river to pray

Step out in faith and be baptized
By grace through faith you're made alive.
Come on down to the river, river
Down to the river to pray.

Let Jesus wash your sins away
Lead you in a brand New Way
Come on down to the river, river
Down to the river to pray.

It's here that we will put on Christ
Walking in the Spirit with a brand new life
Come on down to the river, river
Down to the river to pray.

Buried like him we are today
Raised like him, our third day
Come on down to the river, river
Down to the river to pray.

So we sing with a brand new tongue
Praises to the living One
Come on down to the river, river
Down to the river to pray.

Cover us with a cloud of glory

Being in His presence makes us holy.

Come on down to the river, river

Down to the river to pray.

PRAYER AT THE BAPTISMAL SITE: Oh Lord, we come to the river as you did. We rejoice that in you we are washed and made as pure as snow. Our baptisms call us to be your children. Help us, oh Lord, to fulfill the ministry you have for us. In the name of Jesus. Amen

21. JERICHO

Scripture: Mark 10:46-52

When you mention Jericho it seems we immediately remember "the walls come a-tumblin' down" or "Joshua fit the battle of Jericho." In the archeological park at Jericho in the Palestinian Authority you will find remains of a tower dating back 7000 years. Other walls and towers show that Jericho, an oasis, has a long history. Present day Jericho will boast of Elijah's Springs in I Kings and even the sycamore tree in which Zacchaeus waited for Jesus. If you believe it's the exact tree I have some swamp land in Florida I can sell you. On the other side of modern Jericho is where New Testament Jericho can be found. The ruins of small homes and large palaces of King Herod can be found.

Jericho is a place where faith made a difference. In Mark 10:46 we find Bartimaeus, the blind beggar. His affliction of blindness has robbed him the ability to work and so he begs. He is totally at the mercy of others. When Jesus comes to town, Bartimaeus begins to cry out so Jesus will not pass him by. He uses the name Jesus, thou Son of David, in Mark 10:47. Bartimaeus is calling out in faith. He had a faith that was waiting and hoping for Messiah. Another name used for Messiah was the Son of David. Faith had begun to flow. When Jesus calls for him, Bartimaeus again demonstrates his faith. He casts off his cloak in verse 50. The garment that he jettisons was the beggar's cloak that identified this man as being one among the poor and needy. Casting aside the cloak, Bartimaeus believes that coming into contact with Jesus will change things. And when he meets Jesus he tells Jesus clearly that he desires to receive his sight and it is done.

In life we need to learn the lesson of Bartimaeus. We must use the faith that is within us. Look around you for the encouragement of faith because of what God has done in your life before this. Remember, that's not just having a flashback, but reliving the events where you have seen God at work. For Bartimaeus, was it Joshua and the children of Israel taking the town? Or was it the transformation that had occurred in the life of that tax collector, Zacchaeus? What are the faith events that encourage you?

Likewise, be ready to act on your faith. Leaving behind his garment was a sign of Bartimaeus's faith in action. It's always good to have the faith that God has placed in each of us and to be growing that faith. But faith is given to be used – to step out believing that the Lord will meet us and do the great miracle that is needed in our lives. Faith can be a noun but most of the time it is a verb. When we are using our faith, it is pleasing to God.

I had gathered in the home of a Jewish believer in Jesus, along with several other believers. We sang our praises from the Psalms and then read the selections for the week from the Tanak, the Jewish Old Testament. Then we read from the Testament of Yeshua, the New Testament. After hearing the Word and meditating on what the Lord had for us in it, one of the men in the group, Avraham spoke up and said that he felt that the healing spoken of in the reading about Bartimaeus was for him. By faith he spoke out that he believed that he was healed of the cancer that had been within his body for the past three years. Avraham told us that he was going to the doctors who were treating him and ask for an MRI to see what had happened. When he saw his doctors he spoke again from his faith that he felt he had been healed. When the test results were in, the doctors were amazed. Avraham showed no sign of cancer in his body. Because Avraham was willing to use the faith he had, to claim the word of God for him, and he was willing to walk by faith, he saw the cry of his heart answered. Using your faith, can you hear Jesus asking you the same question that he asked Bartimaeus, "What wilt thou that I should do unto thee?" (Mark 10:51).

PRAYER AT JERICHO: Jesus, open our eyes that we might see your wonder and power as you touch our lives. May we offer sight to a world gone blind in the name of Jesus. Amen.

22. JERICHO ROAD – WADI QELT

Scripture: Luke 10:30-37

The parable of the Good Samaritan, perhaps one of the best known of Jesus's parables is set along the Jericho Road. The road that is still seen and can be walked today winds its way from cliff to cliff around the Judean Mountains from Jerusalem to Jericho. The Roman road has lasted for over 2000 years. In many places along the route the road is filled with switchbacks so that you cannot see what's ahead of you until you are right on it. Thus the setting of the story immediately filled the minds of the hearers with fear. For along this road there were known to be bands of robbers, so no one would travel alone if at all possible.

Yet the man who "fell among thieves" (Luke10:30) was looking for trouble. He had disregarded every precaution that a good Jewish traveler would take. When he is robbed and his clothing taken, his hearers would have said he deserved it.

The travelers who come upon the robbed and beaten man were the normal users of the road. Levites and Priests were always walking here as Jericho was the home to a group of the Priests. Luke 10:31-32 have the Levite and Priest coming down the road. What difference does that make which way they were traveling? A lot, for it means that the excuses usually used to justify their behavior, i.e., that they are going to the temple to serve their appointed time of service, or that they cannot become defiled so they can't go to the temple to teach, are taken away. They were not trying to keep pure, as they were simply heading home. Their shunning of the man was totally selfish. The final character in the story – the Samaritan – would be a man who normally would not be found on this road, as it was used by Jews to avoid Samaria and Samaritans. It was the bypass road for Jews from Galilee going to Jerusalem. Likewise, the Samaritan, if returning home, is going the wrong way. From Jerusalem to Samaria is only 18 or 19 miles north of Jerusalem and this road is south of the city. The fact that the Samaritan stops, helps, takes the man injured to an inn, and pays the bill for his care all cause great consternation for those who heard this. These are the things the Law of Moses commanded and yet here a Samaritan, one worse than the dogs, does what is commanded and is called "GOOD."

One life lesson is to remember that this is a parable. It is a story, not an event that actually happened, but one that is told to get a point across clearly. Jesus used stories. How many times do we miss Christ's teaching because we no longer have time for the stories we hear in life. Christ can still teach if we have ears to hear.

We also need to heed the point of the story to be a good neighbor and fulfill the second greatest commandment. To love our neighbor as ourselves means when we are faced or aware of a need we are called to do something. I think the story is good for our culture, for often we do a little – write a small check, bring a can of food. But we are called as a follower of Christ to go the extra mile and make sure we are not only treating the surface but the deepest need that those around us have. When was the last time you were a GOOD Samaritan?

PRAYER ON THE JERICHO ROAD: Oh God, ours is a journey of faith. Like the Good Samaritan, our journey is to touch the hurting along the way. Help us to be faithful. Amen.

23. MOUNT OF TEMPTATION

Scripture: Luke 4:1-13

The temptation of Jesus after his baptism takes place in the wilderness. For many of us we think of a dense forest or undergrowth when we picture a wilderness. But the Judean wilderness is quite different. It is barren, arid, rocky, and mountainous. It is the place where all of the prophets and men of God had gone to hear the voice of God and to have their call and purpose confirmed. Moses had gone into the desert and met God in a burning bush. John the Baptist had gone to the wilderness and then came forth preaching. Now Jesus was "led by the Spirit into the wilderness" (Luke 4:1). The place that Jesus went must have been Wadi Qelt. It is the only source of water outside of Jericho in that area. It is rugged and secluded and a place to be alone with God and also to face the Devil. I don't like the wilderness. I want to stay where it is nice and comfortable. Roughing it to me is to stay at the Holiday Inn. Yet, the Spirit led Jesus into the wilderness. Are we willing to heed the Spirit's urging to go to the places where we are not comfortable, to be able to hear not what is easy, but what is godly?

The temptation of Jesus reveals what he is really made of within. The three temptations – to turn stones into bread, be given authority over the world, and be taken to the pinnacle of the temple and be cast down so he would be worshipped – all reveal what Jesus is really like inside. He never takes the easy way out, but will gain all these things – not from the Devil but from his Father, as he is faithful.

At the foot of the Mount of Temptation the stones actually look like the loaves of bread that were baked each day to sustain life. The devil used what was around to taunt Jesus, to try to trick him into using his power for his own gain and to satisfy his hunger. Likewise, the Mount of Temptation is the tallest of the mountains in the area. Was it from here that the devil shows Jesus the kingdoms of the world? Possibly! The final temptation is at the pinnacle of the temple. The pinnacle is located at the southwest corner of the wall around the temple. From this place where the trumpet was blown to remind the Israelites to remember their God, Jesus is tempted to throw himself off and have the angels catch him. If it would happen, the angels would be there since it was the temple.

Using the Scripture he knew from the Tanak, Jesus – the Word – quotes the written word to defeat the evil one. There is no more powerful force in the world than the Word of God.

A life lesson here is to remember that all of us are and will be tempted. Remember that being tempted is not a sign of not being spiritual enough, but is what we can expect when we are encountering God or drawing closer to him. Satan doesn't go after those who are asleep or just normally following Jesus. He doesn't have to do it. Each of us will face spiritual warfare. Battling the Devil and struggling with the temptations in life: "… the lust of the flesh, the lust of the eyes, and the pride of life…" (I John 2:16) will come to each of us. Will we be prepared?

It will take more than a general knowledge of the Bible to fight the good fight and win. We must hide God's word inside of us. We must commit it to memory so we might have a weapon to destroy the Devil when he comes against us. Jesus said, "…in that day the Holy Spirit will bring to your remembrance what you need…" How can he bring to our remembrance what we have never read? Jesus died on the cross so we are facing a defeated foe. Let's rise up and face the Devil and see him run at the name that is above every other name, Jesus.

PRAYER AT THE MOUNT OF TEMPTATION: Oh God our Father, the Spirit drove you into the wilderness to be tempted. May those temptations in our lives give us the strength to face the evil one and destroy him with the word of the Lord and the power of our testimony. Amen.

24. SHECHEM – JACOB'S WELL

Scriptures: John 4:1-42

"He must needs go through Samaria" (John 4:4). The Jewish community would have cringed at that exclamation. A good Jew would never put foot on Samaritan soil. Since the fall of the northern kingdom of Israel in 722 BCE Jews had viewed those in Samaria with contempt. The Assyrian rulers had recolonized the area after taking away the King, his counsellors, the skilled craftsmen, the teachers, and any others who held positions of higher learning. They knew the best way to keep a captured land in line was to bring in persons from other lands of different culture, language, and even culture. The intermarriage of those who lived in Samaria had produced a race of persons not totally pagan but not totally Jewish. Therefore, Samaritans were looked upon with disdain and disgust. This was so true that a Jew going from Galilee would cross the Jordan in the north of the country and proceed down the other side of the Jordan only to re-cross at Jericho. It made a 3-day walk now take 6 or 7 days.

Jesus goes through Samaria and when he reaches Shechum he is tired, hungry, and thirsty. Sending his disciples to secure food and drink, he sits beside Jacob's well. The well is deep and requires one to put down a container to draw water. In the middle of the day, with the sun beating down, Jesus sees a woman coming to draw water. But why would she come in the noon sun when most came in the early morning?

The Samaritan woman and Jesus's discussion leads from the obvious to the personal – from the need to draw water to religion, where to worship, to her marital status or lack thereof. He offers acceptance, concern, and even love for the woman as they share the amazing love of God that breaks down the barriers that humankind put between them. The woman is amazed and is drawn into the Kingdom of God by Jesus. Her life is changed!

Life lesson at Jacob's Well has to do with prejudice and racism. Neither has a place in God's world and especially in the body of Christ. Yet, the ugliness of both is still within the hearts of many. After almost 60 years, racism in the United States and the church can still be found. What can we do about it? It's easy to say it's someone else's problem. However, if we are aware of it we are responsible for doing something about it, like Jesus did at the well. It may be at work or school or in your neighborhood. The change comes only when we help people discover the change of heart that is possible in Christ. When I was in elementary school, integration had just begun. Each year our school held a Celebration on May Day. As part of that day a May Court was elected and a King and Queen were crowned. God has a way of helping us learn the lessons of God's Kingdom. The election of the May Court was held with the King being African American and the Queen being an Anglo. That was one thing. But I was elected part of the court and my escort was Lynette, an African American girl in my class. While not being brought up in a completely racist home my father had made it clear that the races don't mix – ever – no matter what the government said. Internally, I was torn and upset. What to do? This would be a public appearance together. What would that say, just being there? At home there was no question of what to do, drop out. At school, there was the pressure to go through with the May Court as constituted. What to do? I talked to my pastor and he counseled to do what my heart told me. My heart was still filled with prejudice and hatred due to my upbringing. I read the Bible and found in Galatians 3:28 that "In Christ there is neither Jew nor Greek, slave or free, male or female but one body in Christ." The challenge was before me. When I approached Lynette to discuss the quandary I was in, she shared her issue with being paired with a white guy as well. I was surprised, for how could she feel that way about me? There wasn't anything wrong with me – except I was the wrong color. It seemed that we weren't the only ones struggling with this issue. We were seventh graders and it was up to us to work this out. The amazing thing was that of the 15 of us involved in trying to work this out, 10 of us were believers in Jesus. As we talked and shared with each other, God began to change not our circumstance or situation or home pressure, but God began to change our hearts. During that process we saw two of our friends who were the most vocal against going through with African Americans and Anglos together, be changed by the grace of Jesus Christ. On May Day we walked together to the platform and watched our May King crown his May Queen. That day released a spirit of change in Northumberland County not brought about by anything other than Jesus Christ. Where does God want to work through you to bring about change in the social fabric of the world?

PRAYER AT JACOB'S WELL: Like the woman at the well, we are all seeking, Lord. Give us the water that shall never run dry. May the living water of Jesus satisfy our thirst and give life to the world. Amen.

25. BETHANY

Scripture: John 11

At the western base of the Mount of Olives is the village of Bethany. It was here that Jesus would lodge with Mary, Martha, and Lazarus. The family had become a supporter of Jesus and his ministry. They had also become close friends of Jesus.

Bethany today is a Palestinian village. You will find a Roman Catholic Church which has beautiful mosaics of the events that occurred here: Mary and Martha at Jesus feet, dining with Simon, and most famous, the raising of Lazarus from the dead. There have been churches here for two centuries. The present church helps us remember the raising of Lazarus. The tomb of Lazarus is entered not from the church compound but from a public street. How appropriate as a tomb would not have been inside a housing area but away, so that one would not be made impure. There is a long descending staircase down into the depths of the cave tomb. Once reaching the base of the stairs there is a lower chamber in which the body had been laid.

The story of the raising of Lazarus has many interesting twists and turns. When Jesus gets the word that Lazarus is ill he deliberately stays away. John tells us it was to reveal his glory that he did this. As a friend who was like family, imagine what it was like....compassion, empathy, and Jesus's very nature were all held back. How hard that must have been. Jesus is scolded by Martha when he finally arrives. "Jesus Lord if thou hadst been here my brother had not died" (John 11:21). Martha affirms her faith that Jesus is LORD. He could have saved Lazarus from death. You can almost hear Martha's disappointment while trying to keep faith. Mary comes later and expresses the same. Isn't it good to know that Jesus can handle us being honest about how we feel with him? As followers of Jesus we do not have to pretend we feel one way and express ourselves another way. We can be REAL!

The raising of Lazarus by Jesus with the call "Lazarus, come forth" (John 11:43) shows once again the power of him, who is the resurrection and the life. Bringing life to a dead man gives us the miracle that John uses in his Gospel to show that God has broken into human history to reveal his kingdom on earth. The body wrapped in the clothes, which had been placed on him as he was buried, remind us that we too need the power of God to release us from those things that bind us in this life – drugs, alcoholism, illicit affairs, adultery, rage and anger, materialism, and idolatry, just to name a few. When we are bound, we need the community of faith which can help us be ready for the miracle of new life that Jesus is offering.

The life lesson I find here is found in the shortest verse in the Bible, in John 11:35, "Jesus wept." I learned this verse early so that I would always have a verse memorized if asked. "Jesus wept" reminds me that the Savior that I follow was human. Weeping is a very natural emotional response. It is alright to allow ourselves to feel and express our emotions. Being a follower of Jesus does not make us immune to human emotion. It isn't a lack of faith to experience them and show them. But Jesus here reminds us, not only is it OK to share these feelings, but the very Son of God is touched and affected by life's situations along with me. I think as I stand at Lazarus's tomb – be real and you will see the resurrection power of God released.

PRAYER AT BETHANY: Father, help us to be like Mary and soak in your presence. Help us to be like Martha to do the work that you have for us. Let us abide in Bethany oh Lord. In Jesus's name. Amen.

26. DOMINUS FLEVIT

Scripture: Luke 13:34; Matthew 23:37

The church shaped like a tear drop is the place to remember Jesus weeping over Jerusalem. Half way down the mountain, the view of the Holy City is magnificent. Looking at it is a testimony to man's desire to worship the Lord God of Abraham, Isaac, and Jacob. In the place where the Jewish temple once stood, you would think that Jesus would be rejoicing after the acclamations of the crowds on Palm Sunday. But Jesus is moved so deeply realizing what is before him – the cross – that he cries out from deep within. He weeps! Weeping, because as often and in every way possible, God has been reaching out to his chosen people and yet they have consistently and continuously killed the prophets and all those sent to them.

The mosaic on the altar of the church illustrates a hen gathering her chickens. Jesus, like so many times before, uses an image the people knew, a mother hen (Matt 23:37). He likens God's actions to a mother hen caring for and protecting her chicks by gathering them under her wings. The sadness of Jesus is heard when, after telling them of God's caring desire to be a part of their lives, their world, he says, "But you would not." The saddest words – you would not.

Dominus Flevit, the church of the tear drop, proclaims that we can break the heart of God. We have the freedom to choose to follow God's plan. But we also can refuse and turn away.

I use to live life thinking that I had been given the gift of choice in life. And my choices only affected me. Crazy, right? But do we realize that what we choose affects God. Choices are important and what we do affects the heart of our God! One day when visiting the church on the Mount of Olives I meet a young woman. She was sitting on the wall looking at the city of Jerusalem. I sat down and introduced myself and she told me her name was Victoria. She was twenty something, from the UK. Victoria had made a lot of decisions in her short life. Many of them had not brought her what she was looking for at all. She realized that her decisions had broken the hearts of her parents and family. She was bumming around the world doing whatever she had to in order to survive. After having been inside the church she had come outside and was dealing with what she had seen and read inside. On the altar she had seen the hen and chicks. But more so, she had read how Jesus wept here. She was so moved when she realized that Jesus was weeping for what others had done. She said "I've caused him to weep over and over by the things I've done. Funny, it never mattered who I hurt before but that I did this to the Son of God. Wow! I have to do something." We talked for a long while about what she might do. As I watched her walk away I thought "Lord how many times do I make you cry?" Does it make a difference when you realize you make Jesus cry, even today?

PRAYER AT DOMINUS FLEVIT: Jesus, you are like the mother hen who cares for her chicks. Keep us under your wings and protect us from all harm. Amen.

27. GARDEN OF GETHSEMANE

Scripture: Luke 22:39-44

At the base of the Mount of Olives lies a church surrounded by olive trees. The Church of the Agony of Jesus or The Church of All Nations is one of the most historic spots in Israel. The church with its ancient olive trees in a garden, murals of the events in the Garden of Gethsemane, and the dark stained glass window give you the feeling that you are there on that fateful night so long ago.

Gethsemane means the "place of the press." Here was an ancient olive grove and it was the place the olives were pressed. Olives give up the precious oil within, only when put under great pressure and weight. The night before the cross when Jesus comes to the garden he had frequently used for prayer, he is weighed down. He asks the disciples to keep watch and pray with him. He goes a little way from them and falls down and prays with such passion that Jesus sweats great drops of blood. The stress of what lies before him, the cross, the betrayal, the beatings, and the physical pain cause Jesus to feel the press. What Jesus is really made of, as a human, is seen here when he says "Let this cup pass from me; but not my will but thine be done."

Jesus, even in the press and stress of life's issues, was willing to be obedient no matter the course.

In life, the lesson we learn from Jesus here is you can't run from the stress. So close to the Judean wilderness, Jesus could have escaped the pressure and his future cross by simply running away. As uncomfortable as the press might be, we never escape it by running away.

When we are in the midst of being pressed we must keep the proper attitude of faith. Jesus expressed how he really felt – I don't want to suffer but not my will but THINE be done. It must always be about God's will. We are never happy or fulfilled in our walk of faith until we are in the center of God's will, even if that is in the press.

When my wife and I were not able to have children of our own we sought to adopt a child by a private adoption. All went well until we got home with the baby and the birth mother of our son, Joshua, exercised her right under Virginia law to ask for the baby back within the 15 day waiting period. I discovered what the press was like. I had never known what pain and agony could come. I prayed fervently for God to change the situation and return Joshua. However, I had to make a choice. Would I submit to the will of God or not? I didn't understand God's will at that time. Now I have come to understand that out of the press, I learned to be able to submit even my hopes and dreams to him. Since that time, God has used my experience in the press to minister to couples who have lost a baby the same way I had. When I stand at the casket of a child, God allows me to feel the pain as that family feels it, for I understand loss. Submitting to the press isn't usually what we want, but it is the only way to show what's inside of us and to be usable by God.

When you are in the press God sends his angels to care for us (Luke 23:43). God will not leave us when we need him most. He sends the resources we need to go "through the valley of the shadow" (Psalm 23: 4). Never be afraid – God will provide!

PRAYER IN THE GARDEN OF GETHSEMANE: In the darkness we seek your will. In the olive garden we face the press. Reveal what we are made of and the oil that gives us light for the darkness. Amen.

28. BETHPHAGE

Scripture: Matthew 21:1-11; 18-22

Bethphage means "house of figs." It is a small village on the ridge called the Mount of Olives. It is to this village that Jesus sent his disciples to find a donkey for Palm Sunday. Was the meeting regarding the donkey prearranged or was it simply another miraculous event? I'm not sure. But I am sure that the owner of the donkey was blessed because he made him available for the use of the Lord.

The other event in the life of Jesus which takes place near Bethphage is the encounter of Jesus with the fig tree. Jesus is hungry and as such goes to the fig tree to find something to eat. Mark 11:13 gives another detail to this story when it says that "…he found nothing but leaves, for the time of figs was not yet." Jesus then curses the fig tree and later it is found withered. The detail Mark includes seems to call into question the act of cursing the fig tree for having no figs if it wasn't the season. The fig tree in the Middle East would leaf out in the spring. It would then develop small nodules at the base of the leaves. Many would take the nodules, suck on them and gain refreshment from them. The nodules were a sign of what kind of a crop you would have at harvest season. When Jesus came, he was looking for the nodules. Not finding them, he knows there will not be fruit later on in the growing season. So he curses the tree.

Jesus ends the encounter at the fig tree by stating, "Verily I say unto you, If ye have faith, and doubt not, ye shall not only do this which is done to the fig tree, but also ye shall say unto this mountain, be thou removed, and be thou cast into the Sea; it shall be done." Jesus used the withering of the fig tree to teach a lesson about faith. He refers to this mountain. Is he referring to the Mount of Olives or Moriah or Scopus or all mountains in the area? I don't think so. I am convinced that the mountain Jesus is referring to is a mountain in the distance called Herodian. King Herod, in building his fortress Herodian, cut off the top of a mountain outside Jerusalem and hollowed it out and built his place to escape. He had workers level another mountain nearby to make his fortress even more impregnable. I think that Jesus is referring to the fortress made by man that wasn't to be breached. Likewise, he is talking about the physical mountain that was used as the base for Herod's construction.

Three life lessons are found here for us. First, Jesus needs what we have. Like the boy with the lunch in Galilee and the owner of the donkey here, what we have is needed by Jesus. Often we need to remember that, even though what we have may not be all we think we need or good enough, Jesus still needs what we have. Are we willing to give to Jesus what we have?

Second, there is judgment coming if we are not bearing fruit. Our faith walk is often bluster and show and not producing the fruit of the Spirit. We look like a follower of Jesus, people think we are a follower of Jesus, but the fruits from our lives do not show it. Examine yourself and see what fruit you have been producing. Judgment does come and it is real, so be prepared.

Third, by faith we can move mountains! All of us face mountains in our lives. Some by our own making and some by the making of outside forces. But when we exercise the faith God has given us, when we speak forth faith and wrap the faith in God around us, we will see that mountain disappear from our lives. Walk and speak in faith and see the wonders of God!

PRAYER AT BETHPHAGE: Father, may we be like the donkey – always ready for your use. And may our lips be filled with Hosanna! Blessed is he who comes in the name of the Lord. Amen.

29. MOUNT OF OLIVES

Scripture: Acts 1:1-11

East of the city of Jerusalem is a range of mountains called the Mount of Olives. From the precipice of the Mount is a beautiful panoramic view of Jerusalem. Pilgrims coming to the temple from the south would crest the mount to get their first glimpse of the Temple of God. It was like a blazing light on a hill. Today it is still breathtaking, as you see not only the Holy Temple, but the Dome of the Rock, a shrine of Islam with its golden dome.

The Mount of Olives is the sight of many events both in the Old and New Testament. David flees from Absalom out of Jerusalem here, the Shekinah – the glory of God, leaves the Holy of Holies and abides here for a time. This is the place of sacrifice of the red heifer on the Mikphad altar, the only sacrifice done outside the temple precincts (Numbers 19). Jesus mounts the donkey on Palm Sunday here, the crowds line the road and lay down their garments and palm branches. Jesus weeps over Jerusalem and teaches the Lord's Prayer here.

Jesus leads his followers out of the city and comes to the ridge of the Mount of Olives. He reminds his followers that they must remain in Jerusalem until they receive the

Holy Spirit. The Spirit will give them power to become witnesses. The Ascension of Jesus from the Mount leaves us with a promise. Zechariah 14:4-8 says, "And his feet shall stand in that day upon the mount of Olives, which is before Jerusalem on the east, and the mount of Olives shall cleave in the midst thereof toward the east and toward the west, and there shall be a very great valley; and half of the mountain shall remove toward the north, and half of it toward the south. And ye shall flee to the valley of the mountains; for the valley of the mountains shall reach unto Azal: yea, ye shall flee, like as ye fled from before the earthquake in the days of Uzziah king of Judah: and the Lord my God shall come, and all the saints with thee. And it shall come to pass in that day, that the light shall not be clear, nor dark: but it shall be one day which shall be known to the Lord, not day, nor night: but it shall come to pass, that at evening time it shall be light.

And it shall be in that day, that living waters shall go out from Jerusalem; half of them toward the former sea, and half of them toward the hinder sea: in summer and in winter shall it be." The promise the Angels give is the same promise.

When Jesus returns to earth he will return to the Mount of Olives. The prophecy goes on to say that when Jesus returns, there will be an earthquake which will split the

Mount of Olives and release pure living water – water that will transform the arid Judean hills and the Dead Sea. The amazing thing is that the Mount of Olives is a natural watershed. From the Mount, rain water flows to the Mediterranean Sea and the Dead Sea. The living water according to the prophecy will transform the Dead Sea and turn the Ahava, a region near the Dead Sea into a green, fruitful place from which teaming life is found in the Dead Sea. This is the beginning of the transformation of earth.

The life lesson on the Mount of Olive starts with claiming the promise of the Angels, "….as you see him go He will return." Jesus will come again. We are called to live as a people waiting for the promise of Jesus's return. It is easy to become bogged down in the deteriorating morals and culture we live in. But the eternal hope that is ours is Jesus is coming and when he does he will change the desolate places into a fruitful oasis in our lives. Jesus coming again is the hope that the best is yet to come.

PRAYER AT MOUNT OF OLIVES: We rejoice, oh Lord that you are coming back to earth. Let us be ones who see you come and touch down on the Mount of Olives to fulfill the prophecy of the end times. In Jesus name. Amen.

30. BETHESDA

Scripture: John 5

The pool of Bethesda was located inside of the Lion Gate and north of the Temple Mount. It was a pool that was known for its healing properties. Around the pool were five porches, covered areas where the sick and the infirm could come. There was a legend that if you entered the waters of the pool after the angel had "troubled or moved the waters" you would be healed (John 5:3-4). So, there were people who came or were brought to the pool and would wait and wait and wait, hoping for a miracle. The physically disabled man of 38 years was one of these.

Why did Jesus pick one out of the many? Why this particular paralyzed man and not another? The reason will never be known except that it was for the glory of God and restoration of health. Ultimately, the work is done to draw others to see the glory of God. God is among us and he is still doing great and miraculous things.

Jesus asks the man, "Wilt thou be made whole?" (John 5:6). The man explains why he hasn't been healed. He is alone. No one is there to help him get into the water. After 38 years he is on his own. Jesus speaks and commands him to "Rise, take up thy bed and walk." And he does and he walks.

The question Jesus asks the paralytic man is the life lesson for us – what do you want me to do for you? Like the paralytic, after 38 years, we are not sure what we need. We learn to live with our ill. We cope with our infirmity. And when Jesus asks us what he can do for us we hesitate. Oh my, well, there's the rent to be paid, the food to be bought, the bank account is overdrawn. In our spiritual life we need to always be ready to lift to Jesus the deepest and most important needs in our lives. What do you need from Jesus today?

PRAYER AT BETHESDA: Heal us, oh Lord! With Jesus we no longer need the stirring of angels but simply the touch of Jesus's hand and we are healed. Amen.

31. CHURCH OF THE HOLY SEPULCHRE

Scripture: Matthew 28:1-10

The Holy Sepulchre Church or the Church of the Resurrection was built by the Roman Emperor Constantine. Helena, the mother of Constantine, wanting to honor her new-found faith, came to the Holy Land to find the places where the Lord had been and done his ministry. Being led by the Spirit and the oral tradition of the early church she identified the sight where a Roman temple had been built during the reign of the Emperor Hadrian. Tradition said that Hadrian had placed a temple to Venus here to cover over the cave where Jesus had been buried. During the construction Helena was said to have found the "true cross of Jesus Christ." While a lot of the things about this site are legend, it is the oldest revered site to remember the death, burial, and resurrection of Jesus Christ.

The Church today is shared by six different religious groups who do not get along. The Roman Catholic Church, the Eastern Orthodox Church, the Coptic Orthodox Church, the Armenian Apostolic Church, the Greek Orthodox, and the Ethiopian Church all have a designated time to spend in the Tomb of Jesus each day. The six denominations do not get along and often even turn to fights over who is trampling on whose territory. As a result, the six denominations cannot agree on almost anything. An example is above the main doors of the church. A ladder was left after some work. The ladder has remained above the doors because the denominations cannot agree on who is to take it down. The inability to agree and work with one another goes so far as to have a Muslim family hold the keys to the church. Each day and night the family opens and closes the church because if not, the various denominations would be in conflict.

There are many chapels honoring many parts of the Resurrection story. One that bears mentioning is the Chapel of Adam. Legend says that Adam was buried here and that the blood from Christ on the cross ran down even onto Adam's corpse to redeem the first Adam by the second Adam. The Chapel of St. Joseph of Arimathea is behind the tomb of Jesus. Here you can see a good example of a first century shaft tomb.

The center of the church is the Tomb of Jesus. Here Jesus was laid after the crucifixion and stayed for three days. Early on Sunday morning an angel came and the power of the Holy Spirit raised Jesus from the dead. He is alive! He is risen! He is risen indeed! From this place sin, death, and the grave have lost their power. Satan and his power have been broken and Jesus becomes the first fruits of the Resurrection. As Jesus was raised so shall we be raised.

A life lesson here is the greatest that we have seen yet. Because of Jesus's resurrection we are children of the resurrection if we are in Christ. Resurrection means that this mortal life is not all there is. We will live forever changed into a resurrection body like Jesus. Death cannot keep us. We are resurrection people and need to live like it.

I often remember how that Resurrection power means that we partake of the Holy Spirit's power and he is dwelling in us right now. (Romans 8:11). The power of Resurrection is in me. I know I am not tapping into very much of that power in my life. How about you?

Likewise, the resurrection reminds me that I will not be alone in this life of faith. We stand in a long line of those who have lived and died faithfully in Christ. The age of the Church of the Holy Sepulchre and the numerous crosses carved by pilgrims through the centuries remind me that we are in a great cloud of witnesses (Hebrews 12:1).

PRAYER AT THE CHURCH OF THE HOLY SEPULCHRE: Alleluia! Christ is risen! He is risen indeed! Alleluia! May the power of the risen Christ raise us up to new life. Amen

32. VIA DOLOROSA

Scripture: Luke 23

The Way of Suffering is a devotional walk through the streets of Jerusalem to commemorate the road that Jesus took to the cross. It begins at Lion Gate and proceeds through the pronouncement of judgment by Pontius Pilate, flagellation, walking with the cross, demanding Simon of Cyrene help carry the cross all the way to Golgotha or Calvary, and Jesus's death. The stations, many based on scripture but some on tradition, are a place to reflect on the passion of Jesus. Whether or not you feel the non-biblical stations are worthy of stopping, the walk itself is one of the best ways to recall the passion of the Christ.

Walking the Via Dolorosa, whether literally or as you move through the scriptures, there is a sense of grief, pain, and agony, as well as hope, because of what the crucifixion was and did. To remember the great pain of being beaten with a cat o' nine tails with bone and broken pottery tied to the ends. To have been jeered and mocked and scorned and taunted as King. Carrying a 90 pound cross beam to the cross through the streets so people could curse, spit on you and throw garbage over you. Only then to have iron spikes driven through your wrists because that's where the nerves are bundled, and severing them would cause the most pain.

Crucified naked so no modesty was left. Struggling to breathe, the one being crucified could not inflate the lungs unless they pushed up on the spike in their ankles and again suffered pain. The punishment designed by the Romans, crucifixion, is still the most painful ever devised by humankind. Cut off and alienated from humankind, emotional pain. And when he cries, "My God, My God, why hast thou forsaken me" – spiritual pain being separated from the Father because God cannot look upon sin. The Via Dolorosa fulfills the prophecy of Isaiah 53. The agony of Jesus is the cost of your salvation and mine.

The life lesson from the crucifixion is the passion of Christ must always be before us. In my study I have a crucifix, Christ on the cross, not because I am a Catholic or do not believe that he is already resurrected, but because I do not want to ever forget the great COST of my salvation and forgiveness. When I see Jesus there I am reminded of what sin does. Many times I sin thinking that it doesn't affect anyone but me and no one knows – so what? However, my sin, private or public always has a cost. It was the agony and passion of Jesus and that doesn't change. I find that when I think of what my sin does to Jesus I stop and think before I act. And most of the time I choose to follow Jesus's way and find victory. Walk the Via Dolorosa every time you are tempted to fail and sin. The Holy Spirit will use it to change your life.

PRAYER AT VIA DOLOROSA: Jesus, as we walk our own way of suffering give us the courage to be faithful. Let your Holy Spirit keep us faithful so we may be a part of the fellowship of your suffering. In Christ. Amen.

33. GARDEN TOMB

Scripture: John 20:1-18

When I first went to Israel I was taken to the Church of the Holy Sepulchre and the Garden Tomb, both claiming to be the sight of Calvary and the tomb of Jesus. The Church of the Holy Sepulchre has tradition and age on its side for authenticity. The Garden Tomb and Gordon's Calvary have the appearance of the skull hill, a rolling stone tomb, and a garden. I will always remember what my first guide told me when I came to Israel. His name was Sari and he said, "Ask me where I believe the tomb was historically and I will tell you the Church of the Holy Sepulchre. Ask me where I want to go and meditate on the empty tomb and what that means? Then take me to the Garden Tomb."

A garden with a new tomb was the only description given in John 20 about the location of the tomb, with the exception that it was close to the site of crucifixion. On that first Resurrection Sunday morning Mary Magdalene finds an empty tomb. That empty tomb changed the world. An empty tomb is the hope of the world. It is a symbol of faith in its verb form and in its noun form. Faith as a noun is seen here because all the rest of what we believe is based on the fact that when Mary got to the tomb it was empty! He was risen just as he said he would be. Faith is seen here as a verb because now we realize faith always involves an action. After hearing the angel's words, Mary goes to the disciples and tells them what she had heard.

The story of the empty tomb in John has a detail not found in the other Gospels. It has to do with the linen napkin about his head being folded and set away from the rest of the grave clothes. There is a story which declares that the napkin which Peter finds folded up is a sign that a person when finished eating would fold the napkin and place it aside, indicating that for them the meal was finished. While this preaches well, in the first century linen napkins were not used at meals. The strips described here were grave clothes. However, the clothes do tell a story. The strips of cloth being folded and set away from the rest of the cloth showed that the body had not been stolen. Who would have stopped to fold cloth when stealing a body? The Greek here gives a picture of the grave cloth being like a glove when the hand has been removed but the glove still holds the shape. Again, proving that the body of Jesus wasn't stolen but miraculously, by the power of the Holy Spirit, vanished out of the strips of cloth and spices.

The life lesson at the Garden Tomb is that the stone has been rolled away. The Resurrection of Jesus moves the stones in our lives. No matter what it is that keeps you from Jesus, the Holy Spirit that raised Christ from the dead will roll it away. Like the first Easter, fear, doubt, unbelief, depression, and broken dreams are all rolled away from our lives in Christ's Resurrection. To allow these stones to stand in our lives is to declare that the Resurrection of Jesus is not sufficient and it isn't complete. But we know that Jesus has overcome and the stones have already been rolled away so we can live in the faith and victory that is ours. I saw Resurrection power in the lives of a young couple in my church. They had hoped and prayed for a baby. God honored their request. During the pregnancy some issues began to develop for mother and baby. The baby was born early and died at birth. How do you help a couple who have had all their hopes and dreams dashed? They were hurting and devastated. I looked at Robert Earl and Loretta and offered them the hope of resurrection. As we held the lifeless form of their son we were able to cling to the fact that one day when Jesus comes, their son would be whole and present to greet them in Christ. We had Easter that day in King's Daughter Hospital's delivery room. In death we are made alive!

PRAYER AT THE GARDEN TOMB: He Lives! He Lives! Jesus is risen from the dead. We claim that same Resurrection power to fill us to follow the risen Lord forever. Amen.

34. MOUNT ZION

Scripture: Luke 22:7-20

In the southern part of first century Jerusalem there was a gate called the Essene gate. The Essenes were a religious group who wanted to purify Judaism and prepare their people for the coming war between light and darkness. It was predominantly a male sect. Thus when Jesus sends two disciples to prepare a place to celebrate Passover and tells them to look for a man carrying a jar of water it most certainly would have put Jesus in Mount Zion.

The Upper Room was the place Jesus instituted the Last Supper, Holy Communion, or the Eucharist. In the midst of the Passover liturgy Jesus deviates and takes bread and says, "Take, eat, this is my body." Then Jesus takes the one of the four cups of the Passover, the cup of salvation and says, "Take, drink, this is my blood of the new covenant." I do not believe that Jesus meant literal flesh and blood but I do believe when we receive the bread and juice that the Spirit of Jesus is received!

"Do this in remembrance of me" says Jesus. Remembering doesn't mean to simply sit passively by and think, but it means to actively relive this event every time you do it. In the Communion, we encounter the living

Christ by faith as we eat the bread and drink the cup. It is a spiritual supper.

The Upper Room is also the place of Pentecost. Acts 2 tells of a rushing mighty wind, tongues of fire, and speaking in tongues. Pentecost is about the fire! The Holy Spirit birthing the church. But more so, the Holy Spirit now poured out for ALL of us to receive. Baptized by the Holy Spirit at Pentecost they proclaimed the mighty works of God to people of all nations.

A life lesson here is that whether it's receiving the Holy Spirit the first time or over and over in Holy Communion we need to constantly be filled by the Spirit. I had a lady in my church who, each Sunday, asked God for more of the Holy Spirit. When Virginia was asked why she asked for the Spirit over and over, she said, "I leak!" I'm like Virginia – I leak and I want more and more of the Holy Spirit in every way I can get it, whether it's by prayer, reading the Bible, the laying on of hands, or Holy Communion. Remember Paul in Ephesians 5:18 says, "be filled with the Holy Spirit." In other words, Pentecost every day!

PRAYER AT MOUNT ZION: Oh God of bread and wine, feed me on everlasting life. Oh Holy Spirit of Pentecost, melt, mold, fill, and use me. In the name of Father, Son, and Holy Spirit. Amen.

35. BETHLEHEM

Scripture: Micah 5:2-3; Luke 2:1-7

Bethlehem means "house of bread." It was here that Naomi returned with Ruth, her daughter-in-law. Boaz and Ruth are married. David is born and chosen as King. Most of all, Bethlehem is known as the birthplace of Jesus the Messiah. Amazing that the Bread of Life should come from the "house of bread." Micah had prophesied where the Messiah was to be born. Amazing that a pagan Emperor would be used to get Mary and Joseph to Bethlehem of Judea to fulfill the prophecy.

The birth of Jesus is believed to have been at the sight of the Nativity Church. Queen Helena built the church based on the tradition that Mary and Joseph came during the census and could not find lodging. They were given the place the animals stayed to have her baby. Most of us think of Jesus being born in a wooden structure called a barn. However, in the ancient world, often houses were built using a cave as a starting point for construction. A family's animals were so precious that often they were kept in the cave near the family for warmth and protection. Mary and Joseph were offered the place of the animals for privacy and to avoid making others ritually impure. The law stated that blood made things impure. It also mandated that being so close to the Temple, a Jewish person must go and sacrifice. If Mary had given birth in the "inn" all of those in the room would be unclean and would have had to wait to be cleansed. Jesus's birthplace in a cave, being laid in a stone manger, an animal feeding trough, gives a glimpse of who he was – the Lamb of God.

The life lesson at the sight of the birthplace of Jesus is that God uses human events to bring his plan into fruition. God used a famine, the death of two sons, and a prophet's announcement over a boy to become King, and even a pagan Emperor. God still uses and works in history. Jesus born in Bethlehem is Lord and King. He is Lord over even the pagan culture of this world. Do not fret or despair. Bethlehem says that God can use anyone, even me.

PRAYER AT BETHLEHEM: Oh come let us adore him, Oh come let us adore him, Oh come let us adore him! Christ is the King of Kings and Lord of Lords. Amen.

36. ST. PETER IN GALLICANTU

Scripture: Luke 22:54-65

After being arrested, Jesus is taken to the house of the High Priest. There Jesus is tried at night, against Jewish law, and held until morning so he could be sent to Pontius Pilate.

In the bottom of the Church of St. Peter in Gallicantu there is a prison. Jesus was probably kept here after his trial before Caiaphas and some of the Sanhedrin who had been handpicked to be there. The prison had no entrance so the prisoner was either lowered down from a hole or dropped down from the ceiling. The prison was originally hewn as a cistern. But the marks on the walls show that it had been used to hold prisoners. Dark, damp, alone, cut off – these feelings only start to describe what Jesus must have felt while in the pit. He knew he was going to the cross to die for the sins of the world. Yet the night before, he had started to experience the emotional angst. Psalm 77 could be David foreshadowing what Jesus would experience in that prison. Did David write a Psalm that Jesus may have meditated on for courage and comfort?

Outside the church is a first century Roman road which Jesus would have walked to get to the trial. Also here, Peter would come to warm himself by a charcoal fire and deny Jesus three times.

The life lesson for all of us is we can easily deny Jesus. Denial is so simple for us. In our culture it isn't popular to confess a relationship with Jesus. So to deny him is often easier than to deal with peoples' reaction. Denying Jesus can be straightforward – "I never knew the man!" like Peter said. But denial is also just remaining silent when others are being ridiculed because of their faith. It's silence when Christian values and morals are under attack. It's silence when others are criticizing and tearing down being Christian. Denial is just as real whether it's the words we speak or the words we do not speak. In what ways have you denied Jesus?

PRAYER AT ST. PETER IN GALLICANTU: Lord, we want to be faithful and follow you no matter what, but we are so weak. Let us learn to accept forgiveness as Peter did on the night before you were crucified. Through Christ our Lord. Amen.

37. TEACHING STEPS OF THE TEMPLE

Scripture: Matthew 23

The Holy Temple in Jerusalem was built by King Solomon, son of David. It was rebuilt by Ezra, Nehemiah, and Zerubbabel after the exile. King Herod the Great expanded the temple platform upon which the temple was built on Mount Moriah. He also renovated the temple building into one of the grandest buildings of the first century in the Common Era. Nothing of the temple building remains on the top of the mount with the exception of a small portion of the wall which separated the Gentiles from the Jewish worshippers.

Jewish worship is centered at the Western Wall. While not a wall of the original temple, it is from the retaining wall of Herod's platform upon which the temple stood. It is holy as it is the closest point which Jewish worshippers can get to the Holy of Holies of the original temple and pray.

Today, in the Davidson Archeological Park there are the temple steps. These stone steps date to the time of the Temple of Herod the Great. The steps are built with short steps and longer platforms. This was done to make sure a pilgrim could not rush into the presence of God. Normally, when entering the temple a pilgrim would be saying the Psalms of Ascent, Psalms 120-134.

The steps were also called the Teaching Steps. Here a rabbi would bring his disciples and teach. In Matthew 23 is an example of what Jesus probably taught seated here. In this passage, Jesus gives a series of "Woe to you scribes, Pharisees, and hypocrites." He compares the Pharisees to white-washed sepulchers (Matthew 23:27). Jesus is basically using an object lesson here – to his left while sitting on the steps was the large Jewish cemetery on the Mount of Olives with its thousands of graves in full view.

The life lesson from the Teaching Steps is the need to slow down and not hurry in the presence of God. Life is so hectic and always on the go that we spend our time with Jesus the same way. To be in the presence of Jesus is not something to be rushed through but savored and cherished. We need to linger and soak in every moment we are with the Lord. In your time with Jesus do you take the time to stop and focus only on him? Learning to slow down with Jesus may just change how we approach life and relationships in it.

PRAYER AT THE TEACHING STEPS OF THE TEMPLE: Jesus you are the great teacher. Give us ears to hear and a heart to do what you ask. Teach us Lord! Amen.

38. EMMAUS ROAD

Scripture: Luke 24:13-35

Where is Emmaus? From within the scripture in Luke there is a footnote in verse 13 that gives an alternate distance to Emmaus from Jerusalem. Is it found at Abu Ghosh, Latrun or El-Qubeibeh? We can never be sure where the village is located but we do know that sections of the Old Roman Road can be found traveling west from Jerusalem, especially near the modern city of Motza. Construction over 2000 years old is still in place and passable.

I believe that the road to Emmaus can be found wherever more than one of us gather to discuss the Scripture and desire to meet Jesus. As Cleopas and the other disciple are traveling west from Jerusalem they are engrossed in conversation. The afternoon sun was in their eyes and the miraculous report of the women who had been with Jesus was causing lots of questions and discussion. A stranger approaches and joins the conversation and then "And beginning at Moses and all the prophets, he expounded unto them in all the scriptures the things concerning himself" (Luke 24:27). Emmaus is always found when people are discussing and studying God's word. Jesus justifies the events that have occurred by showing the

Scripture that had prophesied the death, burial, and resurrection of Christ the Messiah.

As the day draws to an end, the two disciples invite Jesus to stay the night and break bread with them. Jesus eats with them and takes the bread "blest, broke a few nights before." The words and the order are the same. When they see this act they know that it is Jesus. Immediately, he disappears from their midst and they say "…Did not our heart burn within us, while he talked with us by the way…" (Luke 24:32).

The faith lesson at Emmaus is that when you want to encounter the presence of the living Christ, open the word and the WORD will make himself known. A few years ago I decided that I wanted to see all of the sites called Emmaus. I hired a taxi and for $50 had a driver who would take me to all three sites. First, we went to Abu Ghosh. A crusader monastery church here boasts to have the foundation and water source which would have been at an inn. At Emmaus Nicopolas at Latrun, there is a crusader church ruin with an altar for groups to use for outdoor worship. By the time we drove to El-Qubeibeh it was raining. I told the driver to let me know when we were close to the church. He did and I got out with my faithful umbrella, to walk as the disciples had done so long ago. He tried to stop me, reminding me that I had paid to ride. I told him no, I wanted to walk. He shook his head and said, "Crazy American." I walked until I could go inside the church. I found a wall there from what is believed to be Cleopas's house. Kneeling at the wall, I read the story from Luke 24 once again. After reading I took out a communion wafer, a piece of bread, from the pages of my Bible. I prayed over it and when I opened my eyes I had a Palestinian taxi driver named Abdullah beside me who wanted to know what this thing I had in my hands was. I told him it was a piece of bread which represents Jesus. He said, "Can I have some?" I was surprised! A follower of Islam wanted Communion. All the way back to my hotel Abdullah peppered me with questions about Jesus. The more I shared, I felt my heart strangely warmed. I realized that day I had been to Emmaus driving in a Palestinian taxi. It isn't the site where something happened that is important, that is only to help us remember. The important thing is that we be open because Jesus meets us when we least expect it.

PRAYER ON THE EMMAUS ROAD: Risen Lord, may we, like the disciples on the road to Emmaus, have eyes to see you wherever you may be. Help us especially to see you in the written Word and in bread and wine. In Jesus's name. Amen.

39. SHEPHERD'S FIELD – BEIT SAHOUR

Scripture: Luke 2:8-20

There are three places that remember the visitation of the shepherds by the angels on the night that Jesus was born. All three overlook the hills of Judea and are pastoral landscapes which you would expect for shepherds and sheep. All three have a natural cave associated with them. Caves are plentiful in Israel and many times are associated with spiritual events.

The announcement by the angels on Christmas morning was made to those "watching the flocks by night" – the shepherds (Luke 2:8). They were out in the fields, according to Luke, which means it was early spring. The sheep being tended in and around the town of Bethlehem were special. They were the sheep that were used in the sacrifices during the temple liturgy. God called the shepherds who oversaw the sheep used for sacrifices to come and see the Lamb of God – the Lamb of God who would take away the sins of the world. Was it just an accident that Jesus was born here or was it one more way that God was making known that his son, born of the virgin, was here for a sacred purpose? Even in his birth he is surrounded by those things that point towards his death. The angel makes a point of saying that the baby they were to find was wrapped in swaddling clothes and laying in a manger. The strips of cloth which swaddling clothes were made from were the same as those cloths used to wrap one who was dead. In birth the body was washed in salt, a spice that gave flavor and life. In death Jesus would be wrapped in cloths that were perfumed with frankincense and myrrh. Even in birth, Jesus was announcing he was born to die.

In the church at Shepherd's Field we find Barluzzi construction. The acoustics help to remind us of the message of the angels. For singing in this place you hear, "Fear not: for, behold, I bring you good tidings of great joy, which shall be to all people. For unto you is born this day in the city of David a Savior, which is Christ the Lord. And this shall be a sign unto you; Ye shall find the babe wrapped in swaddling clothes, lying in a manger. And suddenly there with the angel a multitude of the heavenly host praising God, and saying, Glory to God in the highest, and on earth peace, good will toward men" (Luke 2:10-14). The Christmas carols that retell the story "While Shepherds Watched Their Flocks," "Angels We Have Heard on High," and "Hark! The Herald Angels Sing," call us back to adore the Christ child at the manger.

Life lessons – there are many. First, the child of Christmas is the Lamb of God who takes away the sins of the world. So don't make Christmas so sentimental that you forget the child grows to become a Man and fulfills the plan of God. Second, the message of the angels is the message for the world in which we live. Peace and goodwill are absent in so many areas. How can that which Christ has given on Christmas be made real every day? Thirdly, we must, just as the shepherds "…go even unto Bethlehem and see this thing that has come to pass…" (Luke 2:15). When we hear of where God is at work, we don't wait for him to come to us, we must go to him.

PRAYER AT SHEPHERD'S FIELD: Lord may even we, the lowliest of your followers be faithful to your Word and seek you as you are born in our hearts. Care for us great Shepherd of the sheep. Amen.

40. POOL OF SILOAM

Scripture: John 9

Many sites found by archeologists are purely accidental. Eli Shukron shared with me that he was making a routine inspection where a drainage pipe was being installed. After checking the site, Eli was turning to leave when he heard a backhoe scraping rock. He stopped everything and started to wipe away the dirt to reveal stone on stone. Had Eli been ten minutes sooner or later everything may have been destroyed. Coincidence? I don't think so. I'd say God-incidence. It was the Pool of Siloam, discovered in the Silwan neighborhood of Jerusalem. The discovery of the Pool of Siloam simply proved the veracity of Scripture once again.

Jesus sees the man born blind and reaches out to heal him. He uses the most unorthodox methodology. He spits on the ground, makes mud, puts it on the blind man's eyes and tells him to go wash in the Pool of Siloam. The blind man does so and begins to see. Imagine the wonder and excitement of seeing the sky, birds, flowers, trees, and even people for the first time. No wonder when the religious leaders start to question and argue over what Jesus had done, the formerly blind man says, "all I know is once I was blind but now I see" (John 9:25).

What was Jesus thinking? Why didn't he simply speak and restore sight? He could have laid hands on and touched the man's eyes to restore his sight. But Jesus made mud pies and put it on the blind man's eyes. In the first century there was the belief that spit/saliva had curative power. It was a medical treatment for blindness. I think Jesus chose this treatment to show us that no matter what method is used, all healing comes from God. No matter whether it's the hands of medicine or the hands of prayer, God is still doing the healing.

The life lesson of the Pool of Siloam is very real to me. God is still in the healing business. God will heal his own. In 2017 I had a stroke which paralyzed my left leg, arm, and side of my face. When I got to the emergency room I wasn't able to speak clearly. I was scared. My deepest fears had been realized – a stroke. The doctors decided to give me a clot buster drug, TPA. It was explained that if there was a bleed in my body I would bleed out and die. My wife, Mary Dale and I prayed. I said yes, believing that as we had prayed God could and would use any method he wanted to heal. After receiving the drug I was a little better and the doctors said that would be all that I could hope for – a life not speaking clearly and paralysis. As I laid in bed that night I prayed and prayed asking God to finish the healing work that the doctors had begun. I saw a beautiful light come to the end of my bed and as the light came up and over my feet, legs, torso, arms, and my head I felt life and strength come back into my body. I began to praise God for what the light of his glory had done. When the nurse came in to take my vitals I sat up in bed and extended my arm and said, "I think you will be needing this." She looked at me and said, "You can't do that you've had a stroke. It says so right here." I said, "You're right. I did, but Dr. Jesus picked up where your doctors left off." Jesus healed me completely. He did use the TPA but when it had done all it could do, Jesus finished the healing completely and totally. Remember, Jesus heals so don't be afraid to ask so that God's glory might be made known.

PRAYER AT THE POOL OF SILOAM: Lord Jesus, help us to wash in the water of the Word! Wash us so that we might be clean and acceptable to the Lord of the Temple. Amen.

41. HERODIAN

Scripture: Matthew 2:1-12

The Herodian is a fortress that was built by Herod the Great about 12 miles from Jerusalem. Herod was appointed King in Jerusalem by Rome. He was an Idumean and not even a Jew. Thus, Herod was seen as a usurper of the throne. This fact only made a man who was already paranoid more so. As a result, King Herod was always worried about who was plotting to overthrow him from his throne. His paranoia would lead to two things. The first was the murder of some of his wives and sons. It was said in the ancient world it was better to be one of Herod's pigs than his family. The second thing his paranoia would lead to was Herod becoming a massive builder. He built cities like Caesarea Maritima to endear himself to the Emperor of Rome. He enlarged and rebuilt the temple in Jerusalem to win favor with the High Priest and the Jewish people. Herod also, not fully relying on being able to win favor by building, constructed a series of fortresses around his Kingdom so that no matter where he was there was a place to flee in the event of an uprising. Each fortress was equipped with food, water, weapons, and a garrison for protection. Herodian was one such fortress.

Herod chose to build the Herodian by cutting off the top of a mountain and hollowing it out, building the fortress down inside of the mountain. Another mountain was close by and for security reasons Herod had it leveled for fear it could be used to stage an attack against the Herodian.

Being not far from Bethlehem it is highly possible that King Herod was at the Herodian when the Magi or Wise Men reached Jerusalem. The Magi or astrologers from the East had come seeking the great King who had been born. It was believed that when a great man or ruler was born it was shown in the heavens – a star was born at the same time to announce the arrival. Having seen the star, the Magi journey, probably not alone but in a large group, for they were men of power and riches so servants would have come. That would take time to gather the caravan and then to journey to Jerusalem. So when they arrived and Herod asked when the star appeared, and then killed all the children two and under, it was because probably as much as two years had elapsed since the birth of Jesus. Was it at Herodian that a paranoid King would become so afraid of an infant King of the Jews that he would resort to infanticide? The fortress didn't give the security to Herod that he thought. The Wise Men leaving and not returning as they had been instructed angered him. The fear that the child was the fulfillment of an ancient prophecy of a Messiah to come overwhelmed and threatened what he held most dear, his power. Herod behind his walls of security lashed out at the vulnerable and lowly.

The Magi finding Jesus in a house, another reason to believe that time had elapsed, bow down, worship and offer gifts. Gold was the gift for a King. Frankincense was the gift for a priest. It was used in the sacrifices of the temple. Myrrh, a spice used in the burial process, was used for one who was to die. These three gifts symbolized Jesus ministry.

What life lesson can we learn from astrologers or a paranoid King? No matter our station in life, Jesus still demands a response from us. We can never be passé about Jesus. Whether a threat because of our lifestyle or a newborn King who deserves our fullness of worship, we can never just ignore him. We have to respond. So how are you responding to Jesus in your life?

PRAYER AT HERODIAN: Almighty God, you use even the evil ones like King Herod to fulfill your prophecy. May we be sensitive to all around us to see your hand at work. Amen.

42. MOUNT OF EVIL COUNSEL

Scripture: Matthew 27:3-30

The Mount of Evil Counsel is the name of the mountain where the United Nations is headquartered in Jerusalem. What irony that this site is also where the High Priest and others met to decide what they were going to do about Jesus. His popularity was growing. His ministry among the people was creating whispers and even shouts of "save us" and "He is the Messiah!" What would and what could they do?

It was from that meeting on the Mount of Evil Counsel that the idea was formed to seek someone who might give Jesus into their hands so that he might be killed. As Caiaphas the High Priest had prophesied, it is better one person die instead of a whole nation (John 11:50). The gospels say that Judas asked them what they would give him to betray Jesus into their hands. One explanation of what happened is that Judas was simply a pawn in the plan of God and had no choice in what he had to do. I do not think that's true. I believe that Judas still had a choice in the matter. Another possibility is that Judas was trying to force Jesus's hand in declaring himself as Messiah. Never really believing he would ever be killed, but at the last minute he would set aside the Romans and usher in an earthly kingdom.

After seeing Jesus going to the cross Judas repents of what he has done. He throws the blood money – 40 pieces of silver, the price of a slave – back at the High Priest, goes out and hangs himself.

Judas serves as our life lesson here. He repents of what he has done. But he doesn't accept the forgiveness that is ours and was his. John 1:9 says, "If we confess our sin, he is faithful and just and will forgive us of sin and cleanse us from all unrighteousness." It is often easy to cry out in our pain and repent. But it is hard to accept forgiveness and to believe that God really does want to forgive us. Not only that God wants to forgive us, but that God will forgive us. I find that often God forgives me, but I can't forgive myself. We need to beware, for we do not want to be like Judas. His actions showed that he felt he knew more what was required for forgiveness of sin than God did. The root of sin raises its head – we act like we're God and supersede what he says. Just think, if Judas had accepted the forgiveness of Jesus after repenting, what a witness for Christ he would have been. God wants to forgive more than we want to ask. So live as forgiven and reconciled for that is the fruit of repentance.

PRAYER AT THE MOUNT OF EVIL COUNSEL: Oh God, may we never gather to plan ways to hinder your work. Forgive us Lord. Amen.

43. DAVID'S CITADEL – KING HEROD'S PALACE

Scripture: Mark 15:1-15

It is always so amazing that in Israel when you are sure you have discovered what a site actually is, someone digs a little further and something else turns up. At the Citadel of David inside of Jaffa Gate in the old city of Jerusalem a recent discovery has challenged the location believed to have been where Jesus was tried before Herod Agrippa and Pilate the Roman military governor. Pilate did not reside in Jerusalem but in Caesarea Maritima, the Roman capital of Palestine. Pilate did come to Jerusalem for the religious festivals of the Jews. He wanted to take personal charge of his troops when Jewish nationalism was running high, as it always did during the high Holy Days. He also wanted to hear firsthand what the itinerant rabbis were saying, as almost all came to Jerusalem for the large crowds. When he came it has been assumed that Pilate was at the Pritorium, a massive Roman garrison overlooking the temple. However, would Pilate, a politician from Rome not take advantage of the finer things in life when able? Herod's palace would have offered the finer things such as what riches could buy for royalty. It is known that in the palace Herod had a large swimming pool – and we thought we had a monopoly on indoor pools. But more, Pilate would have had the opulence of a royal throne room to intimidate the High Priest and the

Sanhedrin. The trial of Jesus was probably here in Herod's palace. The judgment seat or Gabbatha, the pavement or place of judgment has been found.

The life lesson here at Herod's palace and the Judgment Seat is "what shall I do with Jesus?" (Mark 15:12). For Pilate, Herod, you, and me – we must answer that question. Pilate tried to ignore it and then pass it off on Herod. Herod sends Jesus back to Pilate because he doesn't want to get involved. As I stood at the Judgment Seat I came face to face with that question. In my own life I have found sometimes it is easier to send him away. Push Jesus aside because his presence hinders what I want to do.

It is always easier to try and cast our decision for what we will do with Jesus to others. Like Pilate, we want other people, as he did with the crowd, to decide what we will do with Jesus. When we do, we escape bearing responsibility for the decision or so we think. The only real option in life is to embrace Jesus as Savior and Lord. To give him full control of our lives. And to put ourselves at his disposal and not the other way around.

PRAYER AT DAVID'S CITADEL: Like Jesus, who stood here before Pilate and Herod Agrippa, may we be faithful even in the face of death and hardship. Keep us faithful, oh Lord. Amen.

44. JUDGMENT SEAT – GABBATHA – LITHOSTROTOS

Scripture: Matthew 27:15-31; John 19:1-13

At the beginning of the Via Dolorosa there is a museum called the Lithostrotos. It is here that archeologists have found a portion of the original road and courtyard that Jesus would have walked on the way to Golgotha or Calvary. The pavement is ribbed as it would have been in Roman construction to allow for proper drainage from the rain. It has the normal large flagstones which the Romans used. If you look closely you can see there have been figures and shapes carved into the stone. The shapes were used for a game among the Roman soldiers called Kings and Jackals. This was probably the game that was being played when Jesus was being spat upon and dressed up like a King.

In the place of Judgment, Pilate sets up a choice. Desiring to release Jesus, Pilate decides to use an old custom of releasing a prisoner at the Jewish festival. The act was a pitiful nod at honoring the religious festival of the Jews, Passover. Pilate brings forth a notorious prisoner named Barabbas. He was a murderer and probably a part of the group called the Zealots – Nationalists who were leading a counter insurgency against the Romans. So Pilate presents Barabbas whose name means bar – son and abbas – a man, or son of a man. Jesus is presented to the crowd as well. He is the Son of Man. A choice is then given – release Barabbas or Jesus. The crowd was choosing between the son of a man or the Son of Man. One a mere mortal whose choices in life had not been good. He was a man of hate and death. Jesus was the Son of Man. Son of Man is a messianic title which all the Jews knew. It meant that this man was the one sent from God. He would save his people and set them free from their captivity. And the crowd chose Barabbas. Jesus was sent to crucifixion.

The life lesson here is that all of us will have to choose between a son of a man or the Son of Man. So often we choose the son of a man who is the weekly flavor being given the limelight in the media. Or the latest sports professional becomes our role model only to discover that he has committed adultery or is an alcoholic. To choose a son of man is a dangerous thing. But to choose the Son of Man is to find life. When Jesus is Lord of our lives he brings a life full of passion, possibilities, and peace. Who have you chosen?

PRAYER AT THE JUDGMENT SEAT: In the moment when we must choose what we will do with Jesus, let us lift him high and give glory to the lamb that was slain. Amen.

45. 1st CENTURY STEPPED STREET/ DRAINAGE TUNNEL

Scripture: John 7

The amazing nature of our faith is found above ground and below ground. Shortly after discovering the Pool of Siloam, Eli Shukron discovered a first century street and drainage tunnel that ran from the pool up to the Temple Mount, completely intact and completely underground. The layers of dirt that have accumulated since the time of Jesus have buried much of what can teach us. Discovered here was a dagger or sword from the time of Jerusalem's destruction in 70 ACE. Also a golden bell, possibly from the bottom of the High Priest's robe has been found. Man uncovers what time has covered so that the Scripture might be uncovered more fully by the Holy Spirit.

This street would have had a special use during the Feast of Tabernacles. On the last day of the feast there was an ablution or cleansing of the temple. It was symbolic of the prayers for and belief that they would be answered for the former and latter rain. The High Priest and other priests serving in the temple at that time would go in procession to the Pool of Siloam and draw water that would be passed from priest to priest. When the water arrived at the temple it was poured over the altar, the furnishings, and instruments used in the temple services. With water everywhere, running down and over the temple steps, Jesus stands and cries out, "If any man thirst, let him come unto me, and drink. He that believeth on me, as the scripture hath said, out of his belly shall flow rivers of living water. (But this spake he of the Spirit, which they that believe on him should receive: for the Holy Ghost was not yet given; because that Jesus was not yet glorified" (John 7:37-39).

As I walk through the roads Jesus has left for me I realize that Jesus doesn't leave us alone to walk that road. The life lesson is that the Holy Spirit is given to each of us. He is our constant companion and comforter. Jesus also says that the Holy Spirit will be flowing out of our belly like living water. Living water is that which is moving, bubbling and welling up. It is the kind of water needed for ritual purification, to make us holy. Here Jesus is reminding us that life will be flowing out of us. But not only life but the Spirit as well. For some this overflow is allowing the Holy Spirit to work through you to offer others the life giving water of Jesus Christ to quench the thirst of a "dry and thirsty land where no water is" (Psalm 63:1). For others this living water is speaking in another tongue, as the Spirit gives utterance. The outflowing of the praise of God from our lips and lives offers hope and power to us as individuals in our prayer life. What is flowing out of you?

PRAYER AT THE 1ST CENTURY STEPPED STREET: Jesus, we walk where you walked today. May we be made holy as you are holy when we enter the Holy of Holies through Christ. Amen.

46. HINNON VALLEY – GEHENNA, HELL

Scripture: Luke 12:4-5

Nobody talkin' about Hell but people going there. The Hinnon Valley was the garbage dump for the city of Jerusalem during the time of Jesus. It was a place of stench, decay, and constant burning. Hell, or Gehenna, was a place of uncleanliness. The smell of burning refuse and the decay of garbage had made this place one of revulsion for the Jewish people. But even more than that, the Valley of Hinnon had another reason to be hated and repulsed by a good Jew. Gehenna had been the place where the Canaanites had worshipped the God Moleck. Moleck had the head of a bull and the body of a man. His belly had been hollowed out so that a burning raging fire could be built to consume the sacrifice offered. The God Moleck was demanding. He required human infants as a worthy acceptable sacrifice. Human sacrifice was anathema to the Jewish faith. It is no wonder that Jesus would choose a place such as this to describe and talk about hell.

Jesus warns his followers to not worry about "the one who can kill the body, and after that no more that they can do. But I will forewarn you whom ye shall fear: Fear him, which after he hath killed hath power to cast into hell" (Luke 12:4-5). What an object lesson to paint a picture of this horrible place of fiery destruction and link it to the destruction that awaits all those who do not respond to the saving grace and love found in Christ Jesus.

It is awfully easy to so concentrate on the needs and demands of the present that we forget the eternal. What a life lesson here – to remind us of eternal things – that hell is real and real people go there. It is a place of eternal destruction and revulsion and it is imperative that we not go there but also that others don't go there either. Recently I have had several of my folks at church visit me and talk about the concern that they had for loved ones who they were sure were heading towards hell in the next life. They wanted to do something and so they asked me to talk to their loved ones about eternal things. Heaven and hell. I did and found a great openness to not only talk of such things but interest in the afterlife. Each one to whom I spoke of hell wanted to find a way to avoid that eternal consequence for themselves. Praise God for sinners who had come home to heaven through Christ Jesus. Who do you know who might be in danger of hell or who is already living in hell in this life? So be not afraid, but be open to share saving grace with them.

PRAYER AT HINNON VALLEY: Lord, may we always see Jesus as the only way of salvation, which leads us into eternal life. In Jesus's name. Amen.

47. HOLY PLACE OF MELCHEZADEK

Scripture: Psalm 122:2

In the ruins of the City of David, Eli Shukron has discovered a worship place that dates to the time of Abraham. One room shows where the sacrificial animals were tied before sacrifice. The worship place consists of a room with V-shaped floor, which some believe was for the tables on which the sacrifices were cut up. Another room is an altar and a drain where the blood of the many sacrifices was drained off. Finally, there is a room which contains a white stone stella – a holy stone used by worshippers as a symbol of the god who was worshipped.

In the book of Genesis, after Abraham has won his great victory he offers sacrifices at a place called Salem. Salem = Jerusalem. Abraham gives a sacrifice to Melchezadek, the King Priest of Salem. The archeological date given to this cultic place is the same as given to Abraham in the land of Canaan. Is it possible that this is where Abraham brought his sacrifice? If so, it was also near the Jewish site where their kings were anointed.

PRAYER AT MELCHEZADEK: Lord remind us to always give to you and to be reminded that all good things have come from you. In Jesus's name. Amen.

48. DAMASCUS GATE

Scripture: Psalm 122:2

One of the most ornate and well preserved gates in Jerusalem is from the time of the Ottomans and is known as Damascus Gate. It was given this name because this gate led people out of the city and to the city of Damascus. The beautiful carvings as well as the art work show how important Damascus was as a trading partner.

The ornate construction also shows how important the gate was for protection on that side of the city. A city gate was a place of friendly visitation, commerce, government decisions and the seat of the elders. The seat of the elders was a group of persons who represented the Jewish people. They would make decisions regarding conflicts, property disputes and other issues of the law. The elaborate gate still today serves these purposes.

One life lesson drawn from Damascus Gate is the need for fellowship. Like the ancient world we need those places of community and fellowship. In our world so many of us are isolated from others. From Genesis 1 and 2 our God knew that we needed others. In your day make time for others.

Under the gate we see the ruins from the first century gate. It is very simple but was a part of the second temple wall that was for protection. This gate truly was here at the time of Jesus and it led to the sook or market.

PRAYER AT DAMASCUS GATE: Lord Jesus, let us see our need for others. The time, Lord, we spend with others is a reminder that we are the church. Amen.

49. JUDGMENT GATE

Scripture: Luke 18:25

About 300 yards before entering the courtyard of the church of the Holy Sepulchre there is a Russian Orthodox Church named Alexander Nevsky Church. The Russian church and hostel is named for the 13th-century national hero and saint.

A large city gate was discovered while the church was being built. The gate was believed to be a part of the original wall of Jerusalem during the Second Temple period. The gate threshold stands as the exit from inside the old city of Jerusalem.

There is a legend that the gate was called the Judgment Gate. It was the place where according to the tradition that if a person knew just cause why the sentence upon a criminal was not true, they could come to give evidence, which would then be considered. The twelve followers of Jesus, the disciples, could have presented evidence of the innocence of Jesus but no one came nor said a word. How many times can you speak up for Jesus but end up staying silent? We must remember Matthew 10, "if you will not confess me before men, I will not confess you before my Father who is in heaven."

The gate is also interesting in that to the left side of the gate is the eye of the needle. In Luke 18:25 Jesus said it is easier for a camel to go through the eye of a needle than for a rich man to enter heaven. The eye of the needle has been argued about for centuries. Was Jesus referring to the literal sewing needle? I think not, but think he was referring to a part of a city gate which was called the eye of the needle. Once the main city gate was closed it was not opened until morning. But to the side was an opening which one entered and then had to turn to get into the city. It was just big enough for a camel to get down on his knees and maneuver itself into the city. Jesus was reminding his hearers that a rich man can make it into the Kingdom but it is very difficult because of the love of money.

PRAYER AT THE JUDGMENT GATE: Father in heaven, help us to be faithful to stand up for Jesus wherever we may be. Help us to so keep our priorities on Jesus that nothing, even wealth, would draw us away from the narrow gate. In Jesus name. Amen.

50. EASTERN GATE

Scripture: Acts 3:2

The eastern gate in Jerusalem is also called the Golden Gate, the Beautiful Gate, and the Gate of Mercy. It was the entrance into the Temple Mount from the Mount of Olives.

It was the gate through which the red heifer would be sacrificed so that the temple could be purified. The sacrifice of the red heifer was upon the altar at the end of the bridge which entered the temple complex.

Today the Eastern Gate we see dates from the Ottoman Period. It is bricked up so that the Jewish Messiah cannot enter into the temple through it. Likewise, a Muslim Cemetery is in front of the gate so that whoever enters here would be unclean. Legend says that when Jesus, the Messiah comes the second time he will enter through the Eastern Gate. Dr. James Fleming, an archeologist, was excavating at the gate when there was a cave-in. Underneath the existing gate is the Second Temple gate open and waiting for the Messiah.

One life lesson of the Eastern Gate is the promise and prophecy that Jesus the Messiah will come again and enter into the temple to be proclaimed King of Kings and Lord of Lords.

PRAYER AT THE EASTERN GATE: Jesus you did come and you will come again. Prepare our hearts to receive our King. Amen.